WHEN THE RIGHTEOUS RULE

Bible Positions on Political Issues

When the Righteous Rule: Bible Positions on Political Issues
Copyright © 2004, 2009, 2010, 2020 John Hagee and Global Evangelism Television, Inc.

Written by John Hagee and Sandy Hagee Parker; edited by Dr. David Crockett. Rewritten from *God's Candidate for America*; edited by Connie Reece and Daniel C. Little; produced by Tina Hagee; jacket design by Inprov LLC

Published by: Inprov, LLC., 2150 Continental Blvd., Southlake, TX 76092

Distributed by: Thomas Nelson

Second Edition, September 2020

The Little People ©2000 by Connie Reece. Used by permission.

Unless otherwise noted, Scripture quotations are from the NEW KING JAMES VERSION. ©1979, 1980, 1982. Thomas Nelson, Inc. Publishers.

Scripture quotations noted NIV are from the HOLY BIBLE: NEW INTERNATIONAL VERSION©. Copyright ©1973, 1978, 1984 by International Bible Study. Used by permission of Zondervan Publishing House. All rights reserved.

Scripture quotations marked (NASB) are taken from the New American Standard Bible®, Copyright ©1960, 1962, 1963, 1968, 1971, 1972, 1973, 1975, 1977, 1995 by The Lockman Foundation, La Habra, CA. All rights reserved. Used by Permission. www.lockman.org.

ISBN: 978-1-951701-95-6

CONTENTS

CHAPTER 1

WHEN THE RIGHTEOUS RULE

"A troubled and afflicted mankind looks to us, pleading for us to keep our rendezvous with destiny; that we will uphold the principles of self-reliance, self-discipline, morality, and, above all, responsible liberty for every individual that we will become that shining city on a hill."
–Ronald Reagan, official announcement of his candidacy for U.S. President (13 November 1979)

On June 19, 2020, newspapers and internet news sites around the world carried a shocking image. A one-ton, bronze statue of George Washington—one that had stood in a park in northeast Portland, Oregon for nearly 100 years—was lying face down and covered in blood-red paint and graffiti; the charred remains of a bonfire visible around the head of the statue.

The image of America's revered Founding Father toppled, desecrated, and charred provides the per-

1

fect metaphor for this present moment in America. Indeed, statues of Washington and other key figures of America's rich, remarkable history have been toppled or vandalized in cities across America.

At first, it seemed to some that only Confederate memorials were under attack in the wake of nationwide protests following the tragic, senseless death of George Floyd in police custody. But soon it became clear that it was not America's legacy of slavery that was under assault. It was all of her history, from Columbus to the framers of the Constitution to those who valiantly and successfully fought to end slavery in America.

In other words, it is Western (i.e., *Christian*), civilization itself that is under siege. The same night the statue of Washington was being defiled in Portland, a statue of Junipero Serra, an 18th-century Roman Catholic missionary—one that had stood in San Francisco's Golden Gate Park for over a century—was pulled down and destroyed, as were statues of Francis Scott Key and Ulysses S. Grant.

In fact, throughout that month, statues and memorials celebrating the extraordinary contributions of people like the following came under attack:

- Abraham Lincoln—the Great Emancipator;

- Frederick Douglass—great, black American preacher, abolitionist, writer, and statesman;

- John Greenleaf Whittier—abolitionist

2

and delegate to the first meeting of the American Anti-Slavery Convention;

- Ulysses S. Grant—18th U.S. President and Commanding General of the United States Army, whose strategies were key to the Union Army defeating the Confederacy.

Over a six-week period, at least 183 monuments were defaced, damaged, or destroyed from sea to shining sea, including thirty-three statues of Columbus, nine of the Founding Fathers, and eight of Saint Junipero Serra.[1] It is unlikely that any of those that were damaged and removed will ever be restored. Bit by bit, America's history is being erased.

This is not just an accidental by-product of a season of unrest and political polarization. It is part of a highly orchestrated, well-funded plan. It is a plan rooted in something George Orwell, the author of the totalitarian nightmare novel, 1984, well understood. Orwell once wrote, "The most effective way to destroy people is to deny and obliterate their own understanding of their history." Karl Marx understood this, too. Concerning the overthrow of the Western democracies built upon a heritage of Christianity, Marx wrote, "The first battlefield is to rewrite history . . . Take away the heritage of a people and they are easily persuaded."

That's precisely what has been happening in our once-great nation. The erasure of our heritage and history is merely the initial phase of a longer strategy to overthrow the systems and sacred values that made the

United States of America the greatest place to be born since the Garden of Eden. Yes, I said "sacred" values.

It is no coincidence that this wave of desecration and vandalism was followed by a series of incidents targeting churches and Christian sites. In short order, church buildings in Florida and California were destroyed by fires. A statue of Christ was beheaded in Miami. A statue of Mary the mother of Jesus was beheaded in Chattanooga. The historic St. John's Episcopal Church in the heart of Washington, D.C.—the "church of presidents" as it is known—has experienced repeated attacks and attempts at desecration.

Churches and symbols of the Christian faith are targets precisely because it's impossible to understand the history of the United States apart from the history of Western Civilization, and how that civilization was shaped by Christianity.

In his 2019 book, *Dominion: How the Christian Revolution Remade the World*, British historian Tom Holland proves that much of what has driven the upward progress that we all take for granted was made possible because of the transforming power of the gospel of Jesus Christ. In it, Holland observes, "To live in a Western country is to live in a society still saturated by Christian concepts and assumptions."[2] But that will not be the case much longer if those pulling down statues and spray painting profanities onto holy memorials have their way.

I recount these events not to discourage you but to

challenge you. My aim is not to move you to despair, or even anger, but to action. I point to these developments simply as a timely, vivid reminder of this truth:

Elections matter.

....

When the righteous are in authority, the people rejoice: but when the wicked beareth rule, the people mourn.
—PROVERBS 29:2, KJV

....

Shortly after being elected president in 2008, Barack Obama famously told a group of Republican congressional leaders in a closed-door meeting: "Elections have consequences. And at the end of the day, I won."[3] He did indeed. And his presidency transformed the United States in profound and lasting ways.

Of course, when it comes to elections in this country, we tend to focus the lion's share of our attention on the race for the highest office in the land, the presidency. But the events we are witnessing make it abundantly clear that all elections have consequences—from the White House to Congressional races to the elections of mayors, city councils, and school boards.

For example, police reform became a topic of national discussion in the aftermath of George Floyd's death. And it has not escaped the attention of some that the cities where police reform is most needed and where lawlessness, violence, and chaos run unchecked have city governments that have been under the control of one political party for decades. Those elections had consequences.

Others have noted that those pulling down statues of George Washington and painting the word "racist" on memorials to Lincoln are largely the product of a public education system that long ago abandoned the goal of teaching children the fundamentals of knowledge and instead became a program of indoctrination into Marxist and humanist, anti-American ideologies. We have gone from producing Nobel laureates and entrepreneurial innovators to churning out unemployable, environmentally conscious haters of their own country. Instead of producing builders of towers that reach to the heavens and spacecraft that reach other planets, we have a generation that can only tear down, denounce, and complain.

Perhaps those trivial school board elections mattered, too.

I would never presume to tell you what candidate to vote for. But as a proud American patriot who has personally witnessed a lot of U.S. history across eight eventful decades, I can and will encourage you to vote. And as a pastor and lifelong student of God's Word, I will tell you unapologetically that the Bible speaks clearly to the most critical issues of our time.

The sole purpose of this book is to shine the light of biblical truth on that subject. My aim is to help clarify what the Bible reveals about the pressing political issues of the day, so you, dear believer, can carry that wisdom into the voting booth as you exercise the blood-bought right to choose your leaders.

We can and must reverse the direction of our culture and our governing values. It's not yet too late to do so. But there is no time to lose.

CHAPTER 2

THE FAMILY GOD INTENDED

The family was established long before the
church, and my duty is to my family first.
– D.L. Moody

Since the beginning of time, the family has been the fundamental building block for society. God put man and woman on this earth and told them to "be fruitful and multiply."[4]

God invented the family. Genesis reveals that He created it to be a place of safety, love, nurture, strength, and the foundational unit of civilization. A man and woman, raising children and building a life together was His idea from the very beginning.

A healthy, thriving family was the core building block of God's grand design for our protection, provision, and good. Which explains why the enemy of humanity has spent so much of his time and energy throughout history trying to destroy it. He's still at it. And in the United States of America, he is succeeding.

The forces tearing at marriages and families have never been more fierce. And so much of what plagues us as a society can be traced directly to fatherlessness and the overall disintegration of family life. Not only is the family a building block for society but also for procreation, financial security, and even evangelism.

Without a family, there is no home. Without a positive home life, there is no haven for the strife and pressures of daily living. Satan would love nothing more than for each of us to walk through the valley of death every day. He attempts to do this by stripping you and your neighbors of the enormous benefits that the love and security of family brings.

The core of this building block is the relationship between husband and wife. The power and importance of this divine partnership has been demonstrated through the millennia. And like the family as a whole, marriage has been under constant assault from every side in recent decades. A group of skeptics once asked Jesus a complex question about marriage and divorce in an attempt to trip him up. Jesus's response was to point them back to Genesis. (See Matthew 19:4–6.) We should follow the Savior's lead and do the same.

There we see that God created Eve as a companion suitable for Adam. If Adam could have made it on his own, there would have been no need for Eve. Any student of biography and history can tell you that a man who has achieved great accomplishments has had a strong and mutually supportive wife in his life. Even secular success guru Napoleon Hill, author of one of the great personal goal/achievement books, *Think and Grow Rich*, wrote that one of the major causes of failure in business and personal life is due to the wrong selection of a mate in marriage.[5]

There is a reason why positive contributions made by men without the stabilizing influence of a good woman are very hard to find. Solomon, known as the wisest man of biblical times, agreed with God's assessment that it was not good for man to be alone. Solomon wrote:

> *There was a man all alone; he had neither*
> *son nor brother. There was no end to his toil*
> *yet his eyes were not content with his wealth*
> *"For whom am I toiling," he asked,*
> *"and why am I depriving myself of enjoyment?"*[6]

Just like Adam, the man Solomon described needed a companion, not just to help him through life, but to help him enjoy the fruits of his labor. The husband and wife are the first union necessary to build a family and produce offspring according to God's design. Then the parents and the children together form the basic building block of society. Solomon said that children are a gift from God or a "reward"—the "heritage of the Lord"—and that a man's children are to him like a quiver full of arrows in the hands of a warrior.[7]

Parents have a God-ordained obligation to raise their

children in a godly home according to godly principles, and children have an obligation to honor their parents and care for them in old age, just as the parents cared for the children when they were helpless and dependent. Most of the problems in our society stem from the failure of the family unit to operate as God intended it.

Of course, marriage has been under assault in our culture for decades. Under the Obama Administration, we saw our nation's federal courts, including the U.S. Supreme Court, consistently strike down every attempt by the states to protect the biblical definition of marriage, despite the fact that large majorities of the population favored those efforts. Even the citizens of California passed Proposition 8 in 2008 that defined marriage as being between one man and one woman—approving the measure on a statewide ballot with more than 52% of the vote.[8]

Ultimately, it didn't matter. Just as the court did concerning the abortion issue with *Roe v. Wade* in 1973,[9] the Supreme Court ripped the right to decide this profoundly vital matter from citizens of every individual state in the union with its 2015 *Obergefell v. Hodges* decision. The nation's highest court made it impossible for the citizens of my home state (Texas) or yours, to protect the historical, biblical, common sense definition of marriage.

Like so many disastrous high court decisions of the past, this decision was narrowly decided by 5-4 vote. It serves as yet another powerful reminder that elections matter, and presidential elections enormously.

In a blistering dissent, to the *Obergfell* decision, Chief Justice John Roberts, joined by justices Scalia and Thomas, sternly reminded his five colleagues that their Constitutional role was not to legislate from the bench:

> But this Court is not a legislature. Whether same-sex marriage is a good idea should be of no concern to us. Under the Constitution, judges have power to say what the law is, not what it should be . . . The majority's decision is an act of will, not legal judgment. The right it announces has no basis in the Constitution or this Court's precedent.[10]

In a thundering separate dissent Justice Samuel Alito wrote:

> Today's decision will also have a fundamental effect on this Court and its ability to uphold the rule of law. If a bare majority of Justices can invent a new right and impose that right on the rest of the country, the only real limit on what future majorities will be able to do is their own sense of what those with political power and cultural influence are willing to tolerate. Even enthusiastic supporters of same-sex marriage should worry about the scope of the power that today's majority claims. Today's decision shows that decades of attempts to restrain this Court's abuse of its authority have failed.[11]

Yes, elections matter because the Constitution—that was designed by our wise Founders to restrain the potentially tyrannical power of government—needs to matter. Those restraints are being dissolved in our generation. Justice Roberts closed his dissent in the *Obergefell v. Hodges* decision with these words:

> If you are among the many Americans—of whatever sexual orientation—who favor expanding same-sex marriage, by all means celebrate today's decision. Celebrate the achievement of a desired goal. Celebrate the opportunity for a new expression of commitment to a partner. Celebrate the availability of new benefits. But do not celebrate the Constitution. It had nothing to do with it. I respectfully dissent.[12]

Now more than ever, we must strive to keep the family unit from becoming extinct and stop at nothing to protect marriage as a sacred institution in America, but that tragic court decision made our job much more difficult and set a multitude of other negative effects in motion. As I and others warned back when this battle was being fought, increased "tolerance" for alternative lifestyles will be accompanied by increased "intolerance" for those of us who hold to biblical values and righteous standards.

Justice Alito warned of this very effect in his *Obergefell* dissent!

It will be used to vilify Americans who are

unwilling to assent to the new orthodoxy ... The implications of this analogy will be exploited by those who are determined to stamp out every vestige of dissent. I assume that those who cling to old beliefs will be able to whisper their thoughts in the recesses of their homes, but if they repeat those views in public, they will risk being labeled as bigots and treated as such by governments, employers, and schools ... By imposing its own views on the entire country, the majority facilitates the marginalization of the many Americans who have traditional ideas.[13]

Sadly, that is precisely what we have seen in the five years since that catastrophic decision came down. Christian-owned, mom-and-pop pizza parlors and bakeries have been harassed and bullied out of business for opting not to cater same-sex weddings or events. Often that persecution has come directly from city or state bureaucrats who now have the full imprimatur of the United States Supreme Court backing their actions.

Mainstream Christian organizations have now been labeled "hate groups" by organizations like the Southern Poverty Law Center (SPLC) for holding to the very same stance on same-sex marriage that Barack Obama held right up until he had been safely re-elected for a second term. Because of their opposition to key elements of the LGBTQ cultural and political agenda, Bible-centric organizations such as the ministry of the late D. James Kennedy and Dr. James Dobson's Family Research Council have been placed on the SPLC list of "hate groups" right alongside neo-Nazi organizations and the KKK.

That would be outrageous enough, even if no one paid attention to the SPLC. However, several of the most powerful, pervasive communication platforms and technology giants in America—including Twitter, Facebook, Google, Amazon and others—look to the SPLC for guidance on what is and isn't "hate speech" and identifying "hate groups."[14]

All of this serves to highlight how vital it is to elect public servants who will fight to protect the rights of people of faith and nominate judges who care more about the Constitution than promoting the latest cultural fad.

The battle to preserve and protect marriage as a fundamental building block of our culture is far from over. Which makes it vital that our elected representatives have the courage to not only defend the biblical, historical view of marriage and the home, but also of human beings themselves.

The Next Battleground: Trans Rights and "Gender Fluidity"

"The biggest claim of the transgender movement is that a man who thinks he's a woman can really be a woman, and vice versa. You see this in many ways—from preferred pronouns, sex reassignment surgeries, and demands to use the restroom of perceived rather than given gender. The problem is that this is a philosophical claim that is not true,

and can never be true, in any way or form."
–ANDREW T. WALKER, AUTHOR, *GOD AND
THE TRANSGENDER DEBATE*

The confetti from the celebration parties over their same-sex marriage victory at the Supreme Court had hardly had time to settle to the floor before liberal extremists opened up the next front in their war to remake American society. The next piece of ground they set their sights on taking was normalization of transsexuality and the abolition of the traditional, "binary" male-female distinction.

In other words, after having erased the traditional meaning of the word "marriage," the same cultural forces set about erasing the meaning of the words "man," "woman," "boy," and "girl." Of course, as with same-sex marriage, the initiatives are cleverly cloaked in the robes of tolerance, acceptance, and the protection of "rights." This tends to put opponents of these radical, destructive changes instantly on the defensive, opening them to accusations of being intolerant, hateful, and bigoted.

This means those who would appeal to the Bible, history, common sense, or even just accepted, basic biology, have to spend half their time offering disclaimers and declarations about their motives and methods before they can even begin to make an argument.

Those who buy into the premise of identity politics and what the Gender Studies programs at major universities now call "intersectionality," immediately find themselves in a bewildering, ever-changing maze in which new sexual orientations and genders are constantly appearing.

Of course, homosexual practices have been around since before Sodom and Gomorrah. It's mentioned and condemned in the Bible and acknowledged in the writings of many other ancient cultures. For centuries, the distinction regarding sex and sexual orientation used to be simple and binary. There was male and female. And there was either sexual expression between male and female, as God designed it, or something "other" that existed outside of that design.

In our time, however, homosexuality began to be identified as either Gay and Lesbian—depending upon the gender of the person practicing it—and at some point the popular culture began using the shorthand "GL." Then bisexuals raised their hands and pointed out that they too experienced societal disapproval, but that they didn't really feel comfortable being filed under either label. So, LGB was born, but that didn't last long. The "transgender" community felt left out. LGBT had a relatively long run, but recently that identifier has been judged as hurtfully uninclusive.

For example, groups identifying themselves as "Asexual," "Flexual," "Genderqueer," and other orientations weren't represented in the acronym. A writer with *The College Fix* reported that one liberal college's "Open House" orientation on their website stated that the preferred acronym for maximum inclusiveness had become LGBTTQQFAGPBDSM.[15]

According to the new rules established in the battle over same-sex marriage, each sexual orientation must be acknowledged, accepted, endorsed, and accommodated by our wider society.

Something very similar is underway with the word "gender," which until recently, we called "sex." As anyone who has read the first couple of chapters of the Bible knows, God created two sexes.

....

God created man in His own image...
male and female He created them
–GENESIS 1:27

....

Biology textbooks agree. Except in extraordinarily rare cases where something goes wrong, at the instant of conception, a newly created human being is carrying either XY or XX chromosomes at the cellular level. XY produces a male and XX a female. Nevertheless, the new, "enlightened" thinking demands we believe that "gender is a continuum"[16] —that is, that sexual identity is a spectrum and that there are an infinite number of possible genders.

As a result, there are also now a nearly infinite number of gender pronouns that must be learned and used. We're informed that he and she reflect that outdated "binary" view of gender. Now pronouns such as *ve, xe, ze, zer, xyr* are adopted and everyone else is supposed to know and use them.

This destructive and unscientific approach to viewing human sexuality has already made its way into the popular culture, and is now worming its way into school curriculum across the nation. As with same-sex marriage, those who refuse to embrace it or submit to it, are already being marked for persecution, possibly even prosecution.

Now user profiles on social media sites like Twitter routinely note the person's preferred pronoun. Failing to do so, or simply calling someone born as a girl and who looks like a girl but "identifies" as a boy, "she" can carry serious, career-damaging consequences. That's precisely what Peter Vlaming, a Christian French teacher in a Virginia public school discovered in 2018.

One of his students, a girl who said she identified as a boy, changed her name to a common boy's name and asked to be referred to with male pronouns. Vlaming was happy to call her by any name she preferred because he would do so with any student. But his faith would not allow him in good conscience to lie to himself, her, or others by using male pronouns when talking about a female. The school gave Vlaming an ultimatum: "Use the student's preferred pronouns or lose your job."[17]

The courageous and principled teacher was suspended and ultimately fired. He successfully sued the school district for breach of contract and for violating his First Amendment freedoms of religion and speech.

The more this emerging movement gains traction and acceptance in society, the more bizarre the results become. We see fierce online debates about whether "men" can menstruate.[18] (I'm not making this up!) We see mainstream news organizations twisting themselves into verbal pretzels to avoid using of the word "women" in talking about medical issues such as cervical cancer.

For example, CNN online headline in July of 2020 actually read: "*Individuals with a cervix* are now recommended to start cervical cancers screening at 25 and continue through age 65, with HPV testing every five years as the preferred method of testing, according to a new guideline released by the American Cancer Society."[19] Yes, instead of the straightforward word "women," we get clunky phrases like "individuals with a cervix" to keep from running afoul of the PC police who now insist we all pretend that some people with female parts are actually "men."

It's madness. And the lunacy will continue to escalate unless good people find the courage to stand up and be heard at the ballot box and in the public square. Yes, we will be falsely accused of "hate" and "intolerance." But those doing the accusing will be the same ones currently looking with approval upon violent mobs.

"The first and fundamental responsibility of every Christian is to live by every word that comes from the mouth of God, irrespective of whether our culture makes this easy or hard. This means we need to listen carefully to what the Bible teaches us about human sexuality and gender identity..."
–ROB SMITH, *RESPONDING TO THE TRANSGENDER REVOLUTION*

The Staggering Societal Cost of Fatherlessness

"A good father is one of the most unsung,
unpraised, unnoticed, and yet one of the
most valuable assets in our society."
—BILLY GRAHAM

We hear a lot about "privilege" and advantage from the those who wish to tear down America's great meritocracy and replace it with socialism. What these critics ignore, and what a mountain of research now reveals, is that the biggest privilege a person can be afforded in our nation is to be born into a home with a father that is present and involved.

Young men who grow up in homes without fathers are twice as likely to end up in prison.[20] They are far more likely to engage in drug and alcohol abuse. Having two parents is more predictive of success in life than having money. In other words, according to the Kettering Foundation, "Children from low-income, two-parent families outperform students from high-income, single-parent homes. Almost twice as many high achievers come from two-parent homes as one-parent homes."[21] Another study states that nearly two-thirds of youth suicides; a full ninety percent of homeless youths; and seventy-one percent of all high school drop-outs come from fatherless households.[22]

We now have mountains of research and data that points to fatherlessness and the breakdown of marriage as the primary driver of poverty in America. In testimony before the United States Senate, author and family researcher Barbara Dafoe Whitehead said, "Growing up with both married parents in a low-conflict marriage was so important to child wellbeing that it was replacing race, class, and neighborhood as the greatest source of difference in child outcomes."[23]

> *"Divorce and unmarried childbearing increase child poverty. The majority of children who grew up outside of married families had experienced at least one year of dire poverty."*
> –MARK RANK AND THOMAS HIRSCHL, *JOURNAL OF MARRIAGE AND THE FAMILY*

Nevertheless, we continue to maintain government policies that weaken the family structure, discourage marriage, and, in some cases, actually create incentives for young women to have children out of wedlock.

The inseparable institutions of marriage and family are the key to well-being for all—individuals, communities, and our nation. And yet the forces of "progress" continue to dismantle those foundational pillars of our civilization at every turn.

That includes the institution of motherhood. For several decades now, the idea that a woman might aspire to staying at home to anchor the family and nurture children has been mocked and defamed. The popular culture has told a couple of generations of girls that the only legitimate thing they can desire is to pursue personal satisfaction. Ironically, in an era in which anything and everything must be tolerated, and in which all choices must be respected, the choice to be a wife and mother building a home is considered out of bounds.

For example, Gretchen Ritter, a women's studies professor at the University of Texas, alleges that stay-at-home moms deliver damaging effects to men, women, children, and society as a whole.[24] She states that:

> The stay-at-home mom is bad for society. It tells employers that women who marry and have children are at risk of withdrawing from their careers . . . full time mothering is also bad for children. It teaches them that the world is divided by gender . . . the more stay-at-home mothers there are, the more schools and libraries will neglect the needs of working parents, and the more professional mothers, single mothers, working-class mothers, and lesbian mothers will feel judged.[25]

Not only does this perspective denigrate the holy, historical, and deeply satisfying role of rearing children, it condemns the women who do it. Instead of applauding those who care for our future generations, we are accusing them for being a force for evil in our society.

In summary, the Bible makes it abundantly clear that God created mankind in two distinct, complementary forms—male and female. And that traditional marriage—one man and one woman joined together in loving commitment for life—is God's irreplaceable pattern for happiness and civilization. Any philosophy, policy, or program that would weaken the family is harmful to the common good and must be opposed by those of us who love people and take the Bible seriously.

CHAPTER 3

DEFENDING THE DEFENSELESS

"I've noticed those for abortion have already been born."
—RONALD REAGAN

Abortion

Personhood is properly defined by membership in the human species, not by a stage of development within that species.[26] Yet, ever since the Supreme Court in *Roe v. Wade* ruled that women were free to abort their unborn children, society has attempted to redefine personhood altogether. In Roe, the court held that within the first and second trimesters of pregnancy, abortions could basically be performed at the mother's will. The court went on to say that the individual states can regulate third trimester abortions, if they so choose, as long as provisions are made for both life and health.[27]

The interesting question is, if unborn babies are

not people, then why regulate abortion at all? Why did the court so painstakingly outline what a woman could and could not do in terms of aborting a pregnancy? They did so because the action is not without controversy; they did so because it was a human life that hung in the balance.

Abortion is one of Satan's most sinister machinations: it strikes against the very heart and fiber of what a family is about. For the mother and father of a child to petition a doctor to extinguish its life goes against everything motherhood and parenthood represent. The abortion movement is nothing less than an attempt to format social change to "liberate" women from the obligations, cares, and responsibilities of motherhood. The ubiquitous argument is that "it is the women's right to choose" and prohibiting abortion restricts her freedom to make that choice.

The freedom to choose what? What about the unborn child's freedom? What about their lifetime of choices that is being robbed of them? It is hazardous, for the human race as a whole, when people in power are able to determine whether other, less powerful lives are meaningful.[28]

Although *Roe v. Wade* decimated the civil rights of an entire class of people, this was not the first time they had done so. As previously discussed, the Court, as well as society as a whole, has had a history of persecuting African Americans. In years immediately prior to the Civil War, the Supreme Court decreed in *Dred Scott v. Sanford* that blacks were not as "human" as a white person and therefore could be bought and sold as property.[29] During World War II, the Supreme Court decided it was constitutional to disenfranchise Japanese-Americans of their property and to contain them in what were fundamentally concentration camps for the duration of the war.

Those decisions, along with *Roe v. Wade*, constitute the trinity of Supreme Court disaster. This case held, among other things, that an unborn child was not a person and therefore not protected by the Fourteenth Amendment to the Constitution. (The 14th amendment to the Constitution says that a state shall not "deprive any person of life, liberty, or property, without due process of law; nor deny to any person within its jurisdiction the equal protection of the laws.")

Justice Blackmun's majority opinion stated:

"If this suggestion of personhood is established, the appellant's case, of course, collapses, for the fetus' right to life would then be guaranteed specifically by the Amendment."[30]

The Court went on to say, however, that it was persuaded "that the word 'person,' as used in the Fourteenth Amendment, does not include the unborn."[31] It came down to a matter of nomenclature with the court; the justices held that a fetus was not a person. Randy Alcorn points out that, "like *toddler* and *adolescent*, the terms embryo and fetus do not refer to nonhumans, but to humans at particular stages of development."[32]

Social liberals, who pride themselves in engineering society, would love nothing more than to dissolve the traditional family structure. They believe childbearing, which is the most womanly of functions, represents everything feminists and social revolutionaries wish to eliminate. As quoted by Planned Parenthood of America, "To impose a law defining a fetus as a 'person,' is granting it rights equal to that or superior to a woman's; a thinking, feeling, conscious human being— is arrogant and absurd. It only serves to diminish women."[33] The thinking behind this precept is that if a woman can have the option of sex without pregnancy, then the woman is freed from the domination of men and from the obligations of a home and family.

Protecting the lives of the unborn is not the male-dominated society's attempt to curtail a woman's potential. The pro-life movement is not centered on keeping women in the home "barefoot and pregnant;" they are solely about protecting human life. In Proverbs 31, the ideal picture of a woman is presented. Not only does this woman have a husband and children, but many verses are dedicated to portraying the woman as a powerful entrepreneur.

....

*She selects wool and flax and works with
eager hands. She is like the merchant
ships bringing her food from afar.
She considers a field and buys it; out of her
earnings she plants a vineyard. She sets about
her work vigorously; her arms are strong for
her tasks. She sees that her trading is profitable,*

and her lamp does not go out at night.
–PROVERBS 31:13–14, 16–18, NIV

....

Even two thousand years ago, women not only had a husband and a family, but also had a life of her own that she found fulfilling for herself.

There is no larger issue in America today, no debate that more clearly draws the line in the sand between right and wrong, than abortion. It is a line that demarks a difference as dramatic and obvious as the line between light and darkness. Ever since that fateful day in 1973, when the Supreme Court ruled that abortions were legal, a war has raged between the forces of light (those who stand for preserving the lives of the most innocent and defenseless among us) and the powers of darkness (those who in the name of "reproductive freedom" argue for the right to end the lives of children they deem to be an inconvenience).

God has created all of us as free moral agents. We have the ability to choose between right and wrong. In Scripture, speaking through Moses, God told His people:

....

"I call heaven and earth as witnesses today against
you, that I have set before you life and death,
blessing and cursing. Therefore choose life, so
that both you and your descendants may live."
–DEUTERONOMY 30:19

....

Although God has given us the ability to make our own choices, He is quite explicit about what choice we should make: "choose life." Despite God's direction, Americans today have not been choosing life in staggering numbers. Every year nearly a million-and-a-half abortions are performed in the United States alone; well over thirty-seven million babies have been wantonly destroyed since our Supreme Court rewrote the abortion laws nationwide.[34]

Partial Birth and More

"As any sin passes through its stages; from temptation, to toleration, to approve its name is first euphemized, then avoided, then forgotten . . . first we were to approve of killing unborn babies, then babies in the process of birth, next came newborns with physical defects, now newborns in perfect health."
—J. BUDZISZEWSKI[35]

While Americans have blatantly not chosen life in this matter of abortion, now with our medical prowess, Americans are choosing as to what method they wish to use in ending the lives of their unborn children. James Watson, the Nobel Prize laureate who discovered the structure of DNA, proposed that "parents of newborns be granted a grace period which they may have their babies killed."[36] Furthermore, in 1994 a committee of the American Medical Association suggested harvesting organs from sick babies even before they die.[37] While this may seem like something out of a fiction novel, read the following descriptions of exactly how all of these torturous procedures are executed:

....

For you created me in my inmost being;
you knit me in my mother's womb."
–PSALM 139:13

....

The most common technique used in first trimester abortion is called suction aspiration, or "vacuum curettage."[38] This procedure consists of a powerful suction tube while a sharp cutting edge is inserted into the womb through the dilated cervix. After insertion the suction "dismembers the body of the developing baby and tears the placenta from the wall of the uterus, sucking blood, amniotic fluid, placental tissue, and fetal parts into a collection bottle."[39]

When babies in the womb are as old as 24 weeks, a dilation and evacuation method can be used. Via this method, "forceps with sharp metal jaws are used to grasp parts of the developing baby, which are then twisted and torn away; this continues until the child's entire body is removed from the womb. Because the baby's skull has often hardened to bone by this time, it must sometimes be compressed or crushed to facilitate removal."[40]

Lastly, and quite possibly the *most* disconcerting of all the methods, is what is known as the Partial-Birth Abortion, or a D&X (a.k.a. dilation and extraction) abortion. This procedure is used in women that are 20 to 32 weeks pregnant, sometimes even later into pregnancy.

During this procedure, the abortionist, guided by ultrasound, reaches into the uterus, grabs the baby's leg with forceps, and pulls the baby into the birth canal, feet first, and begins to pull the baby's body out of the mother while the head is left face down in the birth canal. (It is important to note, during this portion of the procedure, the baby is still alive.)

When the baby's body is outside of the vagina and only the head remains face down inside the mother, the abortionist thrusts a blunt, curved pair of scissors into the base of the skull and then opens the scissors to enlarge the wound. After a hole has been made, the scissors are removed, and a suction catheter is placed into the hole as it sucks out the baby's brain and skull contents. After the skull is collapsed, the baby is then fully delivered from the mother.[41]

Dr. Martin Haskell, who describes the partial birth procedure above, said that he had personally performed 700 of these abortions.[42] Although some pro-choice activists would like us to believe otherwise, partial births are more common than we would think. In a news release on November 1, 1995, the Planned Parenthood Federation of America claimed, "The procedure, dilation and extraction (a.k.a. partial birth) is extremely rare and done only in cases when the woman's life is in danger or in cases of extreme fetal abnormality." This allegation has been echoed by pro-choice advocates everywhere, and many people believe that there was truth behind such claims.

This dialogue was rendered moot when the executive director of the National Coalition of Abortion Providers, Ron Fitzsimmons, publicly admitted he "lied through [his] teeth" when he alleged that partial birth abortions were a rare procedure performed only in extreme and rare situations.[43] Fitzsimmons went on to state that he intentionally misled in previous remarks . . . because he feared that the truth would damage the cause of abortion rights.

Additionally, he admitted that although he still supported the procedure, he conceded, "It [abortion] is a form of killing. You're ending a life."[44]

Another argument that abortion advocates attempt to advance is that the fetus cannot feel the pain of these abortions as they are being performed. The truth is, not only can the unborn feel pain, they can feel it more acutely than if they were outside the womb. An expert on fetal pain, Dr. Anad, wrote in his report to the U.S. Federal Court that, "scientific evidence converge to support the conclusion that the human fetus can experience pain from 20 weeks gestation and possibly as early as 16 weeks of gestation."[45]

He then went on to say that the pain felt by a fetus is "more intense than perceived by term newborns or older children" and that the process of partial-birth abortion would result in "prolonged and intense pain experienced by the human fetus."[46] We must realize that these procedures are happening in our country, not Nazi Germany, and they are taking place more often than we think.

It was reported by the National Director of Abortion Providers that, in 1997 alone, between three to five thousand partial birth abortions had been conducted.[47]

....

... "Blessed are you among women, and blessed is the child you will bear! But why am I so favored, that the mother of my Lord should come to me? As soon as the sound of your greeting reached my ears, the baby in my womb leaped for joy."
–LUKE 1:42–44, NIV

....

Another argument that the abortion advocates would like us to believe is abortion is allowable due to the fact that the "fetus" is inside a woman's body and dependent upon that woman's life for survival which means the fetus is not self-sustaining and therefore cannot be considered a life. However, what happens when a woman has a newborn for that matter? If a parent were to leave a one year old in a house by him or herself, could he or she be self-sustaining? Surely not. A child is dependent upon the parent for years after birth in order to survive; dependency does not end as soon as they are no longer in the womb.

Additionally, there have been cases where children were born uncharacteristically early and still survived outside the womb. This was the case with Courtney Jackson, who was born after just 23 weeks into gestation. She was born weighing 460 grams, was 11 inches long, had eight teaspoons of blood in her entire body, and had a heart that was not any bigger than an acorn.[48]

While the odds were stacked against her, the little girl pulled through and lives a normal life today. Pictures of little Courtney's birth should be hanging on the wall of every abortion clinic. It would be a face to the life that they were about to end.

Abortion ends a life, a human life, and it is as simple, as wrong, and as hellish as that. Abortion prevents a future teacher from teaching, stops a future coach from leading. It keeps a doctor from healing and guarantees a future writer will never get a chance to inspire. Abortion is not only a sin against the infant; it is a sin against the future of humanity. Over 40 million putative U.S. citizens have been legally murdered in this country. When will it stop?

The Slippery Slope

"So why do things get worst so fast . . . the usual explanation is that conscience is weakened by neglect. Once a wrong is done, the next wrong comes more easily."
—J. BUDZISZEWSKI[49]

The 2008 presidential election presented one of the starkest contrasts imaginable on the issue of abortion and demonstrated how far down the slippery slope America had descended since the 1973 *Roe v. Wade* decision. During the race between Senator Barack Obama and Senator John McCain, a practice known as "partial birth abortion" became a prominent campaign issue.

Both men had cast votes on a landmark piece of legislation titled, "The Born Alive Infant Protection Act" (BAIPA). The legislation was based upon the reality that occasionally, during late term abortions, the helpless infant actually survives the barbaric procedure and is still alive when delivered. There was abundant evidence that, in those cases, the staff conducting the abortion would then finish the "procedure" by killing the newborn baby.

The BAIPA was drafted to force abortion providers to spare the life of any infant born alive. As a U.S. senator, McCain had voted in favor of this humane and civilized legislation. In contrast, as a state senator, Mr. Obama fought against an Illinois version of BAIPA that was essentially identical to the federal version.[50]

The fact that such a law was considered necessary served to prove what many of us had been warning about for decades. Namely, that gradual societal acceptance of abortion on-demand was a "slippery slope" that would ultimately lead to infanticide. And here we are.

In the same election cycle, a move to end the barbaric practice of partial birth abortion in late-term abortion procedures was debated, with numerous politicians and special interest groups fighting to keep the method legal.

Late term abortion, the abortion of infants simply because they're imperfect (or the "wrong" sex), infanticide, and assisted suicide are all the fruit of the same toxic tree given from the Supreme Court sanction back in 1973. As we've seen, that catastrophic decision was built solely upon the unscientific assumption that the living human being grown in the womb is not a "person." (The very same logic used by an earlier Supreme Court to rationalize slavery.)

CHAPTER 4

WORK, EQUALITY, & JUSTICE

"Nobody is equal to anybody. Even the same man is not equal to himself on different days."
—THOMAS SOWELL[51]

In the opening lines of this book, I mentioned the mobs tearing down the monuments to our nation's founders and calling for the end of police departments, free enterprise, and basically every other aspect of Western Civilization. As those protests and riots unfolded, "justice" and "equality" were among the most frequently used words heard from the apologists in the media and in government who rationalized and defended them.

Those are, indeed, powerful words. Good words. Bible words. Which makes it so unfortunate that they have abused, misused, twisted and hijacked in the service of advancing an agenda that is both anti-American and anti-biblical. That agenda includes a number of elements that run completely counter to the traditional moral framework that enabled the United States to rapidly rise to greatness and become a land of extraordinary opportunity.

Let's explore the true meaning of those key virtues and examine how they are being corrupted by one side in our current cultural conflict.

Work

It's been called an "entitlement mentality" and we've been encouraging it as a culture for some time now. For decades, one side in our current cultural battle has been encouraging people to view government as the source of all blessings and to view as natural "rights" things that can only be earned.

Everything from housing to top-tier medical care to birth control and feminine hygiene products have been declared to be a fundamental "right" by advocates for "social justice" in recent times. We're told that the blessings of abundance and "the good life" that so many in America have achieved over the last two and half centuries should now belong to everyone regardless of talent, character, effort, or sacrifice.

This belief stands in sharp contrast to the work ethic of our forefathers, who in turn were informed by the Word of God.

God is pro-work. He gave the very first man and woman a huge assignment. Adam and Eve had a job to do. Some think that work was a result of the fall, but that's simply not true. Work was and is a key part of God's plan for humanity. In fact, God modeled it Himself in the act of creation—laboring for six days and then resting on the seventh. (see Genesis 2:5, 15) The fall of man and the resulting curse simply made getting results from our labors more arduous.

....

The soul of a lazy man desires, and has nothing;
but the soul of the diligent shall be made rich.
–PROVERBS 13:4

....

The book of Proverbs is filled with exhortations to work hard as well as severe warnings against laziness. It speaks particularly stern language about the tendency to crave luxury and comfort without a corresponding willingness to work diligently.

This principle carries right through into the New Testament words of Jesus. His parable about the three stewards (see Matthew 25:14–30) clearly and powerfully displays the biblical principle that effort and diligence lead to rewards and success, whereas slothfulness leads to the opposite of those things. Jesus closed that parable with these ominous words: "'For to everyone who has, more will be given, and he will have abundance; but from him who does not have, even what he has will be taken away. And cast the unprofitable servant into the outer darkness. There will be weeping and gnashing of teeth.'" (Matthew 25:29–30)

The apostle Paul captured that ethic when he bluntly wrote: "For even when we were with you, we commanded you this: If anyone will not work, neither shall he eat" (2 Thessalonians 3:10).

Today, in flagrant opposition to this immutable principle from God's Word, we find some politicians advocating for something called "universal basic income." This is a program in which the government distributes free money to every resident as a base income, regardless of whether they work or provide any value to society at all.

This program would turn huge swaths of the American public into government dependents and undermine incentives for innovation, risk, and sacrifice.

> *"Easy money had no weight: you didn't feel you'd earned it. What you get for a song you won't have for long, the old folks used to say, and they were right."*
> –ALEKSANDR SOLZHENITSYN,
> ONE DAY IN THE LIFE OF IVAN DENISOVICH[52]

Equality

One of the "self-evident" truths Thomas Jefferson proclaimed in the Declaration of Independence was the idea that "all men are created equal." The founding fathers as a whole embraced this truth and incorporated the phrase into their common vocabulary throughout the war for independence and the founding of the American republic.

But some in our nation have become confused or have been misled about the meaning of that term. The founders had equality of *opportunity* in view—a flat, level playing field where those who work the hardest and the smartest can see how far their efforts can take them.

In contrast, many today are sure that it means equality of *outcome*. That if some people achieve more than others, then it can only mean that something "systemic" created that difference in results.

America's first pioneer settlers came from Europe where class distinctions were deeply entrenched and rigid. If you were born into a certain class, you died in that class.

There was almost no "social mobility"—the ability to rise to a better life through effort, talent, and creativity. But what emerged in the American colonies was something quite different.

Class distinctions were rendered nearly meaningless in the new world. Here, a person could start with nothing and become anything, preserving that freedom from the strict class system; that precious social mobility is what Jefferson and the Founders had in mind when they declared that "all men were created equal."

Of course, there was more to Jefferson's familiar phrase. The full sentence reads:

> We hold these truths to be self-evident, that all men are created equal, that they are endowed by their Creator with certain unalienable Rights, that among these are Life, Liberty and the pursuit of Happiness.[53]

Note that the view was *not* that God had granted us a right to happiness—only the freedom to *pursue* it. Whether you catch it or not is entirely up to you! In other words, no one is born with a right to success and achievement. But we all are born with a God-given right to see what we can make with what we've been given.

Again, this truth lies at the heart of Jesus's parable of the talents and the three stewards in Matthew 25. The stewards were given differing amounts of capital with which to begin investing. But in the end, they were judged not on the total amount of resources in their possession, but rather on how diligently and wisely they had worked with what they were given.

Along these lines, Thomas Sowell, the brilliant black economist and intellectual has written:

> "It doesn't matter how much evidence there is that some groups work harder in school, perform better and spend more postgraduate years studying to acquire valuable skills in medicine, science or engineering.

If the economic end results are unequal, that is treated as a grievance against those with better outcomes, and a sign of an 'unfair' society.

"The rhetoric of clever people often confuses the undeniable fact that life is unfair with the claim that a given institution or society is unfair.

"Children born into families that raise them with love and with care to see that they acquire knowledge, values and discipline that will make them valuable members of society have far more chances of economic and other success in adulthood than children raised in families that lack these qualities."[54]

We hear a lot these days about "privilege." We're assured that the only reasons some groups seem to experience better outcomes than others is that the former are born with advantages that others don't have. There is a sense in which this is true.

As noted in a previous chapter, having a father present in the home is a huge advantage for avoiding poverty, prison, drug or alcohol addiction, and a host of other ills. Having a mother or father that reads to you when you're a child bestows great advantages in success and achievement. Growing up around people who value and esteem education is an advantage as well. And the greatest advantage of all is being dragged by your parents to a Bible-believing, Word-proclaiming, Jesus-exalting church when you're young.

The thing is, all of these "privileges" are gifts every American can give their children irrespective of race, economic status, or background. We are free to choose or reject them. And knowing about the power and value of these advantages is available to every person. They are as close as the nearest Bible.

Once again, Thomas Sowell has a firm grip on this trend as he writes, "Slippery use of the word 'privilege' is part of a vogue of calling achievements 'privileges'—a vogue which extends far beyond educational issues, spreading a toxic confusion in many other aspects of life."[55]

Here is what so few who nod in agreement when some politician is spouting platitudes about equality understand. The only way a nation can guarantee equality of outcome is to become an oppressive, authoritarian regime that punishes initiative, diligence, and innovation while rewarding slothfulness, envy, and resentment. There are those who would transform this nation into that very thing. And they advocate for this by appropriating and twisting a very biblical word. That word is . . .

Justice

The term "social justice" is everywhere these days. It's a stylish phrase. It is not unusual to hear good Christian young people with sincere hearts doing great thing using this phrase to describe their work and mission. In fact, theologically conservative Christian colleges have added Social Justice tracks to their academic offerings. Humanitarian ministries feature the phrase in their mission statements.

What many of these believers don't know is that for decades the term was a core part of the vocabulary of Marxist revolutionaries and Catholic Liberation Theology activists operating in Third World countries. It was used to dress the uglier aspects of Marxist ideology up in prettier clothes. Put another way, it was designed to make a silk purse out of the sow's ear of socialism—ensuring that forced redistribution of wealth, the loss of property rights, and authoritarian government control was more palatable to the masses and more difficult to oppose.

In true Orwellian fashion, social justice became a key fixture in the vocabulary of the academic Left on college campuses all over the nation as a code phrase for messianic, utopian egalitarianism enforced coercively by a god-like State. From there, not surprisingly, it has filtered into the vocabulary of an entire generation of young, idealistic secular Americans; and as we just noted, quite a few Christian Americans as well.

> *"Now, at the end of the second decade in
> the 21st century, something new is hitting
> many of our churches: a social justice
> ideology that is ... anti-biblical, borrows
> heavily from the postmodern worldview
> which aims to redistribute power ...
> and ... is becoming a kind of false religion."*
> –ROBERT OSBURN[56]

As the use of the term "justice" in this sense has spread, the meaning of the term has broadened. So much so, that it is not unusual to hear the fact that one person has more wealth than another person described as a gross example of injustice.

For example, it is not "unjust" in any meaningful sense of the word that the founders of Chick-fil-A have more wealth than you or I. They came by that wealth honestly. They provided a service that people valued. They ran their operation wisely and prudently and prospered as a result. Yet, similar to the confusion about equality of result versus equality of outcome, many people have been taught to view success as a sign of injustice. The word has been hijacked. Here's why that is regrettable.

First of all, "justice" is a very biblical word and you can't read the Bible honestly without coming away with the impression that it is something God cares very much about. However, if you take the time to read all the appearances of the word "justice" in your English Bible you'll find that it carries a very specific meaning— and that meaning relates to punishment of criminal, lawless behavior. In other words, justice is primarily judicial, not economic.

Put another way, a thing can be unfair, unfortunate, or undesirable without being unjust as the Bible conceives justice. The just-ness of a thing depends entirely upon righteous legal and civil codes of law.

"Injustice" in the Bible relates to lawbreakers getting away with breaking the law. Or people being defrauded out of what is rightfully theirs.

Yes, the poor, widows, and orphans are frequently mentioned in relationship to the administration of justice in the Bible, precisely because they can easily get a raw deal in the court system. The wealthy can bribe judges and bureaucrats. The poor can't.

As God makes clear to the Israelites in His detailed instructions on how to set up a civilization: "You shall not distort justice; you shall not be partial, and you shall not take a bribe, for a bribe blinds the eyes of the wise and perverts the words of the righteous" (Deuteronomy 16:19, NASB).

And God said to Judge Moses: "You shall not pervert the justice due to your needy brother in his dispute" (Exodus 23:6, NASB). The Bible also recognizes the danger of justice being perverted due to pressure from populist, democratic demands: "You shall not follow the masses in doing evil, nor shall you testify in a dispute so as to turn aside after a multitude in order to pervert justice" (Exodus 23:2, NASB).

As the Word of God makes plain here, both the rich individual and the poor mob or rioters can influence the judge or jury. In doing so, both pervert "justice."

Contrast this biblical view of justice with the dominant pop culture view that labels any situation in which one person (or country) has more wealth than another as inherently and by definition "unjust."

As we've seen, this view is impossible to square with Jesus's parables about lords who entrust varying financial sums to his stewards, or who pay end-of-day workers a higher hourly rate than all-day workers (see Matthew 20:1–16).

According to the new liberal, pagan culture that is now emerging, true social justice means much more than concern for the lot of the poor. It requires burning hostility toward the wealthy and successful, valuing their destruction as much or more than it seeks the elevation of the poor.

We currently live in a land of people that love to be generous with other people's money. But as the former British Prime Minister Margaret Thatcher once rightly observed about Socialism, " . . . eventually you run out of other people's money"[57]

Equality and justice are important concepts. Which is why it is urgent that we proclaim and defend their true, biblical meaning in the public square.

CHAPTER 5

ATTACK ON CHRISTIANITY

"Congress shall make no law respecting an establishment of religion, or prohibiting the free exercise thereof . . . "[58]

Freedom from Religion

Unfortunately, the principal guilty party in prohibiting the free exercise of religion, a guaranteed constitutional right, has been the Supreme Court. However, Congress is not without blame in regard to the Supreme Court overruling the expressed will of the people. Under Article III Section 2 of the United States Constitution, the Congress has the power to regulate the appellate jurisdiction of the Federal Courts, yet Congress has rarely been so bold to speak out against the judiciary. Those who hail "separation of church and state" and attempt to forbid anything to enter the public sector whose origins are remotely Christian need to realize that the Constitution guarantees the free exercise of religion . . . *even* Christianity.

It is no secret that our forefathers fled England to escape abuse of governmental power.[59] The ideal behind our Republic and the concept of federalism is that most of the control lies with the people and the states; it is not held in a centralized government.[60] The Declaration of Independence shines on the roots of our nation's moral foundations:

> *We hold these truths to be self-evident, that all men are created equal, that they are endowed by their Creator with certain unalienable Rights, that among these are life, liberty and the pursuit of happiness.*[61]

Dr. Norman Geisler, Dean of the Veritas Graduate School in Charlotte, North Carolina, points out that the "Founding Fathers, in accordance with Moral Law, affirmed their belief in (1) a Creator (God), (2) Creation (that man was created), and (3) God given moral absolutes (that man has God given 'unalienable rights')."[62] So why did we depart from our roots?

The shift from the will of the people to the imposition of the will of the court has been a gradual one—this did not happen overnight. It did not explicitly happen when prayer was thrown out of schools, when abortions were made legal, or when the Ten Commandments were removed from public buildings at the insistence of the ACLU.

The seed was planted long before. The problem within our society today is that the majority of our citizens have turned their backs on moral absolutes. There is no right and there is no wrong— everything is relative. Humanism, defined as a "nonreligious philosophy based on liberal human values,"[63] has saturated our society, little by little; and as a result, we are racing down the road to complete and total moral annihilation.

Now more than ever, people seek freedom *from* religion. After all, if there is no God in heaven to decide what is right and wrong, then it is man's perogative to determine right and wrong. It is this philosophy that has increasingly eroded our spiritual rights. Man feels there is no superior authority to his own. With man no longer looking to a deity, but rather looking to himself, he is no longer held accountable by the moral code he once knew. If he can ignore God, he can ignore God's laws such as The Ten Commandments and the Bible. Instead, he permits himself to do otherwise. Never before has there been such polarization between good and evil in our society and the world at large. We are facing a war against Christianity and a cultural war for the soul of the nation.

Mass murder, genocide, and loss of civil rights are no longer stories reserved for Third World countries or history books. We have read of millions being murdered in Nazi concentration camps, yet now we accomplish the same in our abortion mills. We have studied the excess and sexual debauchery of the Roman Empire, yet we have a multi-billion-dollar pornography industry fueled by lust and debased desire. We condemn Middle Eastern governments for forcing their citizens to only worship one god yet attack Christians for wanting to worship their God.

In Psalm 2, a prophetic Psalm, David describes a generation where the leaders of the world rise in revolt against both Christians and Jews. We are that generation. The Word says, "Why do the nations conspire and the peoples plot in vain? The kings of the earth take their stand and the rulers gather together against the LORD and against his anointed, saying, 'Let us break their chains,' they say, 'and throw off their fetters.'"[64]

The focus of this rebellion that David speaks about is God and Christ. The kings of the earth take their stand by "breaking their chains" or the restraints that the Word of God imposes on society. Sadly enough, we are succeeding at doing just that. Look at the worldwide movements whose purpose was and is to cast God out of society: Communism, where the state is the god; Atheism, where there is no god; Secular Humanism, where man is god; and New Age, everything and anything is god . . . except Christianity.

Freedom of religion . . . as long as you are not a Christian

"Nothing that is morally right can ever be politically wrong."
–ANONYMOUS

Many assume that "separation of church and state" appears somewhere in the Constitution. It does not. The first amendment of the Constitution prohibits the making of laws that respect the establishment of religion and prohibit its free exercise. As a result, our lawmakers have made it impossible for public school children to recite Christian prayer in public schools. However, as was reported in December 2003, a California school in the Byron Union School District is requiring seventh-grade students to "pretend they're Muslims, wear Islamic garb, memorize verses from the Quran, pray to Allah and even to play 'jihad games'."[65] A federal judge upheld that such activities were allowable after outraged Christian parents brought a lawsuit against the school district.[66]

While courts are allowing *other* religions to be promoted, Christianity is still being targeted. In May 1995, Samuel B. Kent, U.S. District Judge for the Southern District of Texas, decreed that any student uttering the word "Jesus" at a school graduation would be arrested and incarcerated for six months. His words deserve to be quoted at some length:

> "And make no mistake . . . the court is going to have a United States Marshall in attendance at the graduation. If any student offends this court, that student will be summarily arrested and will face up to six months incarceration in the Galveston County jail for contempt of court. Anyone who violates these orders is going to wish that he or she had died as a child when this court gets through with it."[67]

Unfortunately, this incident is not an isolated one. A teacher at Lynn Lucas Middle School in Willis, Texas shouted, "This is garbage" as she threw two students' Bibles into the trash can. The teacher then took the students to the principal's office, called their parents, and threatened to call Child Protective Services because Bibles were not permitted on school property. Additionally, in that same school, those students whose books had the Ten Commandments displayed on the covers were ordered by school officials to throw them out, alleging that the Ten Commandments were "hate speech."[68]

The attacks don't stop there. When a seven-year-old was asked to bring a book to her classroom show-and-tell to share her Christmas traditions, her teacher barred her from reading it due to the fact that it mentioned Jesus Christ. The teacher said, "Its religious content made it inappropriate."[69] When the school principal was confronted by the child's parents, the principal reiterated that students could "share books about their Christmas traditions so long as those books were not religious."[70]

Another example of this anti-Christian bias occurred in Alabama when a District Court Judge issued an injunction against school prayer. The judge held that prayers were not permitted in any fashion including, "prayers on the school PA system during Veterans Day or times of national crisis."[71] He also went on to categorize students' lunchtime prayers as "disruptive, aggressive, harassing speech by students, even in such a lunch setting, and is not protected."[72]

Another startling example of attack on Christianity took place when Texas Tech biology professor, Michael Dini, refused to write letters of recommendation to medical school for students who would not acknowledge their acceptance of the theory of evolution. Dr. James Brink, the assistant provost, showed support for Professor Dini, citing that students with strong faith and a belief in creationism should not attend public universities.[73]

Regarding higher education, noted history professor George Marsden claims that, "In the most prestigious parts of American academia, religious scholars are given less of a voice than Marxist scholars."[74] Christian Evangelist Chuck Colson had this to say about academic freedom in American universities:

> "We are left with a disturbing paradox. While higher education is better funded and more accessible than ever before . . . it has nothing left worth teaching . . . there is no truth worth pursuing."[75]

These are only a very few examples of how Christianity is being blatantly berated in our society.

Our past presidents have thought education and Christianity go hand in hand. George Washington said, "The future of this nation depends on the Christian training of our youth. It is impossible to govern America without the Bible."[76] Likewise, Abraham Lincoln highlights the importance of education by saying, "The philosophy of the school room in one generation will be the philosophy of government in the next."[77] We must do as the Word says and "train up a child in the way he should go, and when he is old he will not turn from it."[78] However, we have not been training our children in the right way—and in the event that we do not, the state will.

The founder of Secular Humanism, Charles F. Potter, wrote:

> "Education is the most powerful ally of humanism. What can a Sunday school, meeting for one hour a week, and teaching only a fraction of the children, do to stem the tide of a five-day humanistic teaching?"[79]

Many people ignorantly think "secular" means neutral. This is wrong! Secular Humanism is a world-wide religion whose goal is to expel every other faith. As the authors of the Humanist Manifesto delicately state, "We find insufficient evidence for belief in the existence of a supernatural; it is either meaningless or irrelevant to the question of survival and fulfillment of the human race."[80]

Secular Humanism is a non-neutral and religious faith. It is its own religion with its own precepts. The Christian religion is being openly condemned and its symbols are considered illegal. Meanwhile secular humanism is preached and propagated from most public schools and universities.

A huge double standard presents itself. For instance, look to the hypocrisy of the Supreme Court. They open each session with the words, "God save the United States and this honorable court," and chaplains in both houses of Congress open the days with invocations.

One recent prayer from Congress included, "Blessed is the nation whose God is the Lord."[81] The Court made Alabama Chief Justice Roy Moore remove the monument of the Ten Commandments that was in front of the courthouse; however a sculpture of Moses and the Ten Commandments adorns the top of the United States Supreme Court building. The sculpture, entitled "Justice the Guardian of Liberty" by Herman MacNeil, is the most noticeable icon in the entire façade; and interestingly, the Chief Justice's offices are directly behind this portico.[82]

A current prayer in the House reads, "You, Lord, will lead, guide, and direct them in their affairs." The same day the Senate prayed, "Fill our God-shaped void with Your presence and bid our striving to cease."[83] Is this not the same group that prohibits the religious freedoms of their constituents while openly practicing Christianity themselves? Where does our government stand, and why are we allowing this to happen?

The Diluted Constitution

"Do not let anyone claim to be a true American if they ever attempt to remove religion from politics."
—GEORGE WASHINGTON[84]

We can sit and point our finger at the Courts and Congress; however, at the end of the day it is the constituents who are allowing these atrocities against the free exercise of Christianity to be perpetuated. We have stayed mum while pundits and politicians have thrown convoluted reasons as to why a godless society is a better one; yet when faced with the realities of what a godless society entails, we choose to get upset. We must stop accepting their excuses and mandate a change—we must demand freedom of religion for Christians.

Too many times we have heard activist judges and leaders alike who add and subtract from the Constitution as if it were a math problem. How much clearer can the words of the First Amendment be? "Congress shall make no law respecting an establishment of religion or prohibit the free exercise thereof . . . "[85] Yet from that sentence our lawmakers have deduced that God must be ushered out of society. The Constitution has been manipulated to endorse whatever the courts feel is necessary.

Consider the following comparison: when the Supreme Court was asked to rule on constitutionality of the right to abortion, it held that abortions were constitutionally permissible because the right to privacy "is broad enough to encompass a woman's decision whether or not to terminate her pregnancy."[86] Of course there is no "right to privacy" mentioned in the Constitution.

The Court held that this right was found in the "penumbras" or shadows of the document.[87] A right of privacy may or may not be constitutionally acceptable, and the right may or may not have any bearing on the abortion issue—but it has become all too typical for an activist court to work hard to search the "shadows" of the Constitution to discover a right to kill the unborn, yet at the same time restrict freedoms in the face of the explicit injunction to do otherwise.

Lawmakers redundantly resound that it is impossible to know what the framers intended when they wrote the Constitution. While this may be true, the framers did leave some guidelines in regard to constitutional interpretation. In a letter to William Johnson, Thomas Jefferson wrote:

> "On every question of construction (of the Constitution) let us carry ourselves back to the time when the Constitution was adopted, recollect the spirit manifested in the debates, and instead of trying what meaning may be squeezed out of the text, or invented against it, conform to the probable one in which it was passed."[88]

Instead of conforming to the probable meaning of the Constitution, our society continually abuses the freedoms the document was meant to protect. It has already been established that despite the fact that the First Amendment is supposed to enable our freedom to worship, our laws have prohibited it.

Yet in the meantime, all other deviant behaviors—such as burning American flags, torching draft cards, gratuitous use of profanity in public arenas, and glorification of violence—are all acceptable under the scope of freedoms guaranteed by the First Amendment. Allowing this to continue is only going to further cripple the moral foundation of our nation; freedom without "reasonable and responsible limits destroys individual lives and ultimately destroys the fabric of a civilized society."[89]

Some may say that our government cannot legislate morality, but it does so every day. Keeping God out of the picture is not going to stop that from taking place. Does our society not prohibit rape? Is murder not also illegal? What about theft? Our government thinks that it is morally wrong to commit these offenses, thus the government legislates against them.[90] Ironically enough God also "legislates" against these offenses in His Ten Commandments. What is God's reaction to man's efforts to kick Him out? The Word tells us, "The kings of the earth take their stand and the rulers gather together against the LORD and against His Anointed . . . He who sits in the heavens laughs, the LORD scoffs at them."[91] No matter how hard lawmakers try to keep morality and religion out of politics, they will always fail to do so.

If it is inevitable that government legislate morality—that some sort of religious perspective lies at the foundation of our efforts in this republican form of government— then why should we cede the ground to those who hate Christianity? In fact, it could be argued, that "we the people" are the true sovereigns in a republican form of government, and every curse leveled by God against corrupt and perverted regimes in the past will be leveled on us if we do not claim the sovereignty that is rightfully ours!

CHAPTER 6

ISRAEL & THE JEWISH PEOPLE[92]

For this is what the LORD Almighty says: "After He has honored me and has sent me against the nations that have plundered you—for whoever touches you touches the apple of His eye—I will surely raise my hand against them so that their slaves will plunder them. Then you will know that the LORD Almighty has sent me. Shout and be glad, O Daughter of Zion ... "
ZECHARIAH 2:8–10

The apple of one's eye is its center. The prophet Zechariah is declaring in these verses that if you come against Israel and her people, it is as if you have jabbed your finger into the very eye of God. You have not only offended the Almighty, you have also received His full attention.

There are several biblical reasons why Christians should stand with Israel, her people, and their claim to the land.

1. Israel is the only nation on earth created by a sovereign act of God.

Israel belongs to God himself! As Creator of heaven and earth (Genesis 1:1), God has the right of ownership to the universe and therefore can give His land to whomever He chooses. God gave the title deed of the land of Israel to Abraham, Isaac, Jacob, and their descendants forever. (See Genesis 15:18; 17:2–8; 26:3.)

Ishmael, father of the Arab nations, even though blessed of God, was clearly excluded from the title deed to the land as plainly documented in Genesis 17:19–21,

> *Then God said: "No, Sarah your wife shall bear you a son, and you shall call his name Isaac; I will establish My covenant with him for an everlasting covenant, and with his descendants after him. And as for Ishmael, I have heard you. Behold, I have blessed him, and will make him fruitful, and will multiply him exceedingly. He shall beget twelve princes, and I will make him a great nation. But My covenant I will establish with Isaac, whom Sarah shall bear to you at this set time next year."*

Therefore, one can conclude that in God's eyes, the Arab nations have no biblical decree to the land of Israel then, now, and forevermore!

The boundaries of the State of Israel are recorded in Scripture (see numbers 34:2–15; Joshua 11:16–23;

13:1–22). These boundaries are further described in Ezekiel 47:13–23 and all of chapter 48.

When God established the nations of the world, He began with Israel; it is the center of the universe in the mind of God (see Deuteronomy 32:8–10; numbers 34:10–15; Joshua 11:16–22).

The original Royal Land Grant[93] given by God Almighty to Abraham, Isaac, Jacob, and their seed is far greater than the sliver of land presently inhabited by Israel today.

2. Christians owe a debt of eternal gratitude to the Jewish people for their contributions, which gave birth to the Christian faith.

No matter from what nation or people—every Christian owes thanks to the Jews for their spiritual inheritance. Paul is primarily writing to the believers of Gentile origin in Romans, "I am talking to you Gentiles ... " (Romans 11:13, NIV).

Further study of this chapter reveals that Paul distinguishes between the believers of Jewish descent and those of Gentile origin—he never uses Israel as a substitute for the Church.

In Romans 11:30–31, Paul sums up what he has been saying about the responsibility of Gentile believers toward Israel:

Just as you [Gentiles] *who were at one time disobedient to God have now received mercy as a result of their* [Israel's] *disobedience so they too have now become disobedient in order that they* [Israel] *too may now receive mercy as a result of God's mercy to you* [Gentiles] (NIV, EMPHASIS ADDED).

....

God has shown Christians mercy because of the Jewish people and it is now our obligation to show mercy to them by:

1. Demonstrating indebtedness for our faith

2. Expressing unconditional love

3. Praying for the peace of Jerusalem

4. Displaying practical acts of kindness

Jesus Christ, a prominent Rabbi from Nazareth, said, ". . . for salvation is of the Jews" (John 4:22). Consider what the Jewish people have given to Christianity:

- The sacred Scripture

- The prophets

- The patriarchs

- Mary, Joseph, and Jesus of Nazareth

- The twelve disciples

- The apostles

The very foundations of our faith are based on the priceless contributions of the Jewish people. If we love the Savior of our faith, then it is impossible to say, "I am a Christian" and not love the Jewish people.

3. Jesus never denied His Jewishness.

While some try to deny the connection between Jesus of Nazareth and the Jews of the world, Jesus never denied His Jewishness. Jesus told the Samaritan woman in John 4:22, "You Samaritans worship what you do not know; we worship what we do know, for salvation is from the Jews" (NIV). The "we" in this verse refers to the Jewish people. Jesus was identifying Himself with His own people.

Jesus was born to Jewish parents (see Luke 1:26). He was circumcised on the eighth day in keeping with Jewish tradition (see Luke 2:21). He had His bar mitzvah on His thirteenth birthday (see Luke 2:41–50). He kept the Law of Moses (see Matthew 5:17). He wore the prayer shawl Moses commanded all Jewish men to wear (Mark 6:56). He died on the cross with an inscription over His head, "JESUS OF NAZARETH, THE KING OF THE JEWS" (John 19:19).

Jesus considered the Jewish people His family for He said, " . . . 'Truly I tell you, whatever you did for one of the least of these brothers and sisters of mine [the

Jewish people], you did for me'" (Matthew 25:40, NIV). He spoke as one of them.

Jesus is called "the Lion of the tribe of Judah" in Revelation 5:5. The words "Judah" and "Jew" are derived from the same root word. There is no doubt that Jesus identified with the Jewish people during His time on earth and throughout eternity.

If Jesus didn't deny His Jewish roots why should we?

4. God promises to bless those who bless Israel and the Jewish people.

Paul recorded in Romans 15:27, "For if the Gentiles have been partakers of their [the Jews'] spiritual things, their [the Gentiles'] duty is also to minister to them in material things." Time and time again Scripture chronicles the principle of God blessing those that bless the Jewish people.

In Psalm 122:6, King David commands all Christians, "Pray for the peace of Jerusalem: 'May they prosper who love you.'"

Righteousness and peace are destined to spring forth from Jerusalem to all nations of the earth, therefore it befits all people to pray for this Holy City.

Daniel prayed three times each day toward the city of Jerusalem while he was in Babylon. Even though praying was outlawed, Daniel chose to continue to pray and endure the punishment of the lions' den. The Lord protected Daniel for his courage and commitment and intervened on his behalf so he could continue to pray for the City of God.

The scriptural principle of personal prosperity is tied to blessing Israel and praying for the city of Jerusalem. This prosperity is not purely associated with material blessings but to the Lord's favor and protection as well.

5. God judges those who abuse the Jewish people.

The Jews have suffered persecution in many forms and from many different groups of people throughout their history.

One of the major focuses of God's final judgment on the nations of the world will be their treatment of the Jewish people (see Matthew 25:31–46).

The nations of the world will be separated into two categories—sheep and goats.

The "sheep" will be accepted into God's kingdom and the "goats" will be rejected. And the basis for their judgment is given by Christ in Matthew 25:40, " . . . 'Truly I tell you, whatever you did for one of the least of these brothers and sisters of mine, you did for me.'"

Bottom line: the nations that show mercy to the Jewish people will receive mercy from God and the nations that deny mercy to them will be refused mercy.

God makes it abundantly clear in His Word that He will regather Israel to their own land and restore them to His favor. He has also promised to judge the nations and individuals who oppress His beloved people.

....

"For behold, in those days and at that time, when I bring back the captives of Judah and Jerusalem, I will also gather all nations, and bring them down to the Valley of Jehoshaphat; and I will enter into judgment with them there on account of My people, My heritage Israel, whom they have scattered among the nations; they have also divided up My land."
–JOEL 3:1–2

....

A Rising Tide of Hate

In the face of these clear biblical truths and warnings, we are nevertheless witnessing a surge of anti-Israel and anti-Semitic hate in our nation.

Have you heard about the BDS movement? It's global. It's growing. It's insidious. And it's a direct threat to Israel's security. "BDS" stands for Boycott, Divestment, and Sanctions.

The aim of the rapidly spreading movement is to pressure institutions to stop investing in Israeli companies or companies with a significant Israeli presence, and to encourage consumer boycotts of such companies' products.

On college campuses all over the U.S., students are adding BDS pressure campaigns to their annual "Israeli Apartheid Weeks"—both of which seek to demonize Israel while exalting the extremists of Hamas and Fatah as virtuous, long-suffering victims.

As one concerned professor recently noted, at universities all over North America " . . . it's hip to hate Israel."

Pop musicians and other artists who choose to perform in Israel are now the targets of criticism and pressure. The BDS movement represents a destructive tactic in the war on Israel's legitimacy as a nation state. Its goal is to end the State of Israel.

Lest you think I'm exaggerating, here's a recent quote from the co-founder of the BDS movement, Omar Barghouti:

> "If the refugees return to their homes [in Israel] as the BDS movement calls for, if we bring an end to Israel's apartheid regime and if we end the occupation on lands occupied in 1967, including Jerusalem, what will be left of the Zionist regime? That's the question. Meaning, what will the two states be based on?"[94]

The truly troubling thing is that the BDS movement is merely a single element in a wider, deeply anti-Semitic campaign to both isolate Israel and raise suspicions about "Jewish influence" in every nation.

So, it's not surprising to note that this growing movement coincides with a shocking increase in blatant anti-Semitism in the U.S. and around the world. In fact, anti-Semitism is too polite a word for what we're seeing.

It is nothing less than raw hatred for Jews.

For example, in 2014, the global clothing retailer H&M reluctantly pulled a t-shirt from its shelves after receiving numerous complaints. The shirt featured a large Star of David with a demonic, angry skull superimposed over it.[95] The message was unmistakable.

Of course, the roots of this movement—indeed of all anti-Semitism—are spiritual. Satan hates the Jewish People with a blinding hatred. Of course he would, wouldn't he?

As we've seen, the Jewish people are the vehicle divinely chosen through which God delivered the Messiah into the world.

Spray-painted swastikas are appearing with increasing frequency on synagogues and Jewish cemeteries around the world.[96] People in traditional Jewish clothing—even the elderly—are being violently attacked in the streets.

European soccer players are making Nazi salutes ("quenelle" signal) as part of their goal-scoring celebrations.[97] Jewish children are being insulted, harassed, even assaulted.

Yes, the cancer of anti-Semitism—often wearing a mask called "anti-Zionism"—is spreading throughout the world. Yes, it is rooted and animated by demonic forces. Yes, even some well-meaning Christians and Jews have been deceived.

That's why it is vital to elect representatives who will stand against this seductive bigotry.

As I stated in my book, *In Defense of Israel*,[98] the Jewish people have suffered persecution and pogroms; they have outlived Pharaoh's slavery, Haman's gallows, and Hitler's final solution. And I have no doubt that long after Hamas, Hezbollah, and ISIS have been added to the boneyard of human history, and long after the crisis with Iran has been resolved, the flag of Israel will still fly over the ancient walls of the sacred City of David. Jerusalem will continue to be the praise of all the earth and the Jewish people will remain the "apple of His eye" —for Israel lives!

CHAPTER 7

LET YOUR VOICE BE HEARD

"Suppose a Nation in some distant region should take the Bible for their only law book, and every member should regulate his conduct by the precepts there exhibited! ...What a Eutopia, what a Paradise would this region be!"
–JOHN ADAMS, 1756, AMERICA'S SECOND PRESIDENT[99]

What lies ahead?

Scripture has an answer for everything, but what most may not know is that the Bible even has clear and distinct positions on political issues. If we are to live our lives by the Word of God and obey all of His commands, then we must be acutely aware of what is said in that Word regarding the world today. Matthew 5:16 tells us to "let our light shine before men." This New Testament principle presents a profound truth that should be the clarion call for all Christians in America today—to let your light shine. Don't curse the darkness; let your light shine now!

What exactly is meant by such a mandate? Simply this: it's our duty, as Christians, to let the light of the gospel shine in our lives with the power and force that God intended. In a survey by the Pew Research Center, more than 65 percent of the American adult population in 2018 and 2019 claim to be Christian.[100] If this is true, why are we not a dominant force in politics and shaping our country's moral fabric? It does not require profound intellectual insight to understand that our nation is headed down a pathway of moral and spiritual destruction. In the meantime, the church hides the light of God from a world that so desperately needs to be illuminated. Instead of allowing our light to shine through our lives, we sit idly by and curse the darkness we have allowed to perpetuate. When this is the case, the church is not a dynamic force of change, rather it's a mere reflection of the decaying culture around us.

We can change our rotting society and restore it to what God intended. We, the people in these United States, have the responsibility to change anything in our society that destroys the moral foundations on which our nation was founded. Our first objective is to change ourselves and let our light shine as the "city that is set on a hill that cannot be hidden" (Matthew 5:14).

Jesus did not hesitate to call leaders of His day hypocrites—literally, "mask wearers." He was against their showy, superficial, and abhorrent religious pretense. They tried to present a public image completely different from whom and what they really were.

As Christians, we have no right to demand things from our leaders or fellow brothers and sisters in Christ that we do not demand from ourselves. By putting on a false sense of spirituality, we are not fooling God or those around us; we are only turning people away from God. The following are some examples of how Christians can allow these attitudes to rob them of their light.

First of all, you say that you are against abortion, but what do you do to aid young girls in trouble? What does your church do? Do you provide counseling and hope for the future? Do you offer food, medical, and financial support? Or, do you merely cavil against teen pregnancies and judge those who are in such a predicament? When the church offers no alternative, where else are these girls supposed to go but to the world? What are you doing to make a realistic difference in the lives of hurting people facing difficult choices in their own personal abortion debate?

Regarding the issue of homosexuality, the Bible is crystal clear that this act is an abomination to the Lord. In Leviticus 20 the Lord discusses punishments for sin with Moses. Verse 13 records the Lord's view of homosexuality: "If a man lies with a man as one lies with a woman, both of them have done what is detestable..." (NIV). Yet why do we act as though homosexuality or lesbianism is worse than cheating, stealing, being a murderer, or a hypocrite?

AIDS patients are dying painful, impoverished, isolated deaths because they chose a homosexual lifestyle; yet Christians by and large have not figured out that compassion toward sinners in their time of need does not equate to condoning their sin. Jesus is tough on sin, but tender toward the sinner. He died for all of us.

Welfare reform has been a major voting issue ever since President Johnson's Great Society. Put very simply, this "reform" is nothing more than taking money from a man who *will* work and giving it to a man who *will not*. Since that time, over 22 trillion dollars in government aid has been paid out to remove poverty from our society. [101]

Despite this, the percentage of those with incomes under the poverty level has been greater since liberal government activists started taking money from the pocketbooks of those who were working and giving it to those who refused employment.

What is worse, by creating financial incentives to have children out of wedlock, out misguided welfare initiatives shattered the family structure of those in the lower income brackets and has virtually guaranteed generational dependence on government handouts as well as all of the ills that company fatherlessness. Today roughly 100 million of Americans are dependent upon government assistance in some form. [102]

Although the welfare program has been a social and spiritual catastrophe, the Church cannot close its eyes to the truly needy who reside in our midst. While working citizens should not be obligated to finance the lifestyles of those who can work but won't—one cannot assume that everybody in dire economic situations falls in that category.

James wrote, "Suppose a brother or a sister is without clothes and daily food. 16 If one of you says to them, 'Go in peace; keep warm and well fed,' but does nothing about their physical needs, what good is it? 17 In the same way, faith by itself, if it is not accompanied by action, is dead. (James 2:15–17, NIV). When we debate issues like welfare reform, abortion, or transsexual rights, we must remember that those who lack money, have immoral lifestyles, or find themselves pregnant out of wedlock, are not our enemies. Our battles are not with flesh and blood—we are fighting a spiritual war.

> *"Whereas it is the duty of all Nations*
> *to acknowledge the Providence of*
> *Almighty God, to obey his will, to be*
> *grateful for his benefits, and to humbly*
> *implore his protection and favor . . . "*
> —GEORGE WASHINGTON[103]

We have no right to complain about something we have the ability to change. The gospel holds the transforming power of change. In a teaching by John Maxwell he stated, "The problem with the church today is that they don't want miracles, they want magic."[104] He makes a very real observation: while Christians complain about wanting to change our government and crossing their fingers hoping that preborn life will be protected or eager to see the traditional definition of marriage restored and protected—we actually do nothing to see those dreams become reality.

We must not discount the supernatural power of God for one moment; the miracle-working power of God has never ceased. We need to let His supernatural power flow from the Church into our world. "If God be for us, who can be against us?" (Romans 8:31).

Those who prefer to feel inadequate and choose to believe that one person cannot change anything are truly mistaken. Numerous times throughout history the power of one person has changed the masses. Biblically speaking, Esther, just one woman, saved the Jewish people from annihilation. A more modern example is Rosa Parks; her one action, refusing to move to the back of a bus, ignited the civil rights movement and changed our nation forever.

The motivation of one person can indeed change the face of the world. For instance, British statesman Wilberforce dedicated his entire career to ending slavery in Britain in the 1800s. His passion drove him to create a unity among politicians from all parties who endeavored to free the oppressed in their nation.[105] Although Wilberforce and his union were threatened with violence and malignant press and their lives and careers placed in jeopardy, they were not swayed. Wilberforce succeeded and slavery was abolished in his country right before the end of his life. The fortitude and tenacity impregnated in one man gave birth to a new nation.

John Maxwell points out that when a problem is recognized by a few and those few sacrifice to rectify that problem—regardless of the cost—that is when a miracle happens. This is what has changed this nation for the better in the past, and this is what is required in order to incite change in this nation for the future.

We cannot hope that lawmakers do what is right or pray that activist judges have a change of heart. Without "we the people" fulfilling our role in government, the Constitution is nothing more than an antiquated mission statement penned over two hundred years ago.

> *"Our laws and our institutions must necessarily*
> *be based upon and embody the teachings of*
> *The Redeemer of mankind. It is impossible*
> *that it should be otherwise; and in this*
> *sense and to this extent our civilization*
> *and our institutions are emphatically*
> *Christian . . . this is a Christian nation."*
> –U.S. SUPREME COURT[106]

The Constitution is not mere paper from antiquity meant to be seen in museums or read about in history books. It is an active, dynamic document that is as applicable now as it was in its genesis. The same way we reference the Bible in search of spiritual direction, we should reference the Constitution in search of our political freedoms. If we do not use our freedom to defend our freedom, we will lose our freedom.

Nothing appeals to a politician more than intimidated constituents afraid to open their mouths and use their vote. In order to win this cultural war and change our world, we must change ourselves. Do not wait for someone else to tell you how to help. Take the initiative and help those who are in distress. Do not require your leaders to accomplish for society what you are not willing to accomplish in your own life, church, and community.

It is not right to expect change on a greater level if you are not willing to start with the man or woman in the mirror. In order to influence our nation for good in the greatest of issues, we must be living the gospel in the smallest deeds of our lives. A constant theme of goodness must run deep in all of us in order to set ourselves up as representatives of Christ in the political and social arenas.

Solely enjoying fellowship with like-minded believers does not change the lives of the lost. New relationships must be forged. Jesus's answer to this situation is expressed in the book of Luke. He was criticized for associating with sinners, but that did not stop Him: "For the Son of Man came to seek and to save the lost" (Luke 19:10, NIV). Unfortunately, many Christians have translated the admonition "to be in the world, but not of it" (see 1 John 2:15) to mean total and utter separation from the world.

Christians isolate themselves—hoping that the problems in our government and our society will disappear. At best, some are willing to pray about issues, but not willing to tackle them head-on and get involved. That is not to undermine the power of prayer, rather it is being faithful to biblical principles. God is not going to zap all of our problems away when we pray. He expects us to get busy and change the things we can change. That being said, we must engage our culture in the political debate. To do so successfully, we must be able to express ideas in terms the secular world can understand.

We must relate to the debate. One of the great New Testament examples of a Christian engaging in his surrounding culture is when Paul was in Athens reasoning in the synagogue with the Jews and debating the Greek philosophers in the marketplace (see Acts 17:22–31). Because of his compelling secular argument for the gospel, he was able to connect with the world around him in terms *they* could understand and identify. He did not throw Scripture at pagans that did not know the Word; instead, he used their knowledge and beliefs to turn their attention to God.

Today people feast on cable news, social media, and podcasts.

Like the Athenians, our society avidly discusses all the latest ideas and philosophies. But are you able to represent your Christian beliefs confidently when your fellow citizens parrot the latest thing they have heard on *The Daily Show*?

While some decry late-night, fake news shows, at least they attempt to address issues that people are thinking about. We as Christians cannot remain mum on these issues; we must stop letting the television set the terms of debate. Become informed! It is not the truth that will set you free; it is the truth you *know* that will set you free. Learn what that truth is and let your voice be heard.

The purpose of this book is to help you apply your biblical faith to what is happening in your world politically and socially. Letting your light shine means extinguishing the darkness by taking your faith into the secular arena where decisions are being made on issues that affect you and your family. Hopefully, this book has been a jump-start toward engaging the present political culture on the polarizing issues that currently divide our nation, while at the same time equipping you to bring your salt-and-light responsibility as a believer to the public square.

That requires mobilizing a grassroots groundswell of God-believing citizens who bring their influence, values, and servant hearts to the school board, the city hall, the state house—all the way to the Congress, the White House, and the Supreme Court. This involves not just voting, although that is vital, but also getting involved in every aspect of the political process. We must get equipped to make a difference in the governmental, educational, and moral structures of our world.

As you embark on this journey of political engagement, you must always remember that who you are and how you live your daily life will mean more to the people around you than anything you will ever say or any vote you will ever cast. To claim the high moral ground in any political fight, you must be a moral person, living a moral life, fighting a moral cause. You must personify your cause.

The solution to our problems is for the Church to come together in unity . . . to stop fighting each other and start fighting the forces of Satan . . . to speak for righteousness . . . to be as bold as a lion . . . and to take America back—one heart at a time, one home at a time, and one city at a time. More than ever the Church of Jesus Christ must let our light shine upon America!

Your Voting Obligation

How far this nation has come since 1776. Then we were striving for greatness; now we are slipping into a moral sewer. Our national foundations are being destroyed as moral men and women sit by and do nothing. Historical revisionists are rewriting American history, attempting to portray our Founding Fathers as greedy, corrupt, atheistic rebels with nothing to lose.

This could not be further from the truth. Of the 56 men that gathered in the Pennsylvania State House to draw up the Declaration of Independence: 24 were outstanding lawyers, 9 were wealthy land owners, and the 23 remaining were great men of distinction who had a great deal to lose.

These men made a sacred oath to each other, pledging "our lives, our fortunes, and our sacred honor." These men took on the crown of Great Britain; they declared freedom from King George and his taxation without representation. As a result, the King denounced all Americans as "traitors" and ordered them hanged by the neck until dead.

Despite the threat these men still signed the Declaration; John Hancock signed his name so large that it would later become one of the most recognizable signatures in history. You think they had nothing to lose?

Wrong! If they lost their war, they would meet their fate by a hangman's rope. If they won, they would endure years of hardship in a struggling nation.

These men signed the Declaration of Independence with ink and paid with their blood. What would happen to these brave men? Thomas McKean of Delaware was so harassed by the British that he was forced to move his family five times in five months. He served the U.S. Congress without pay while his family lived in hiding and endured poverty. Properties that belonged to Clymer, Hall, Gwinnett, Walton, Heyward, Rutledge, and Middleton were all burned to the ground by the British, just to name a few.[107]

Thomas Nelson of Virginia, after whom Thomas Nelson Publishing is named, raised two-million dollars on his own signature to provision our fighting troops. After the war he personally paid back the loans, which wiped out his entire estate, and he was never reimbursed by the government. In the final battle of Yorktown, Nelson's house was occupied by British General Cornwallis; Nelson urged General Washington to fire on his own home in order to defeat the enemy. Washington complied and the home was totally destroyed. Nelson died homeless, bankrupt, and was buried in an unmarked grave.[108]

John Hart was driven out of his home by the British as he sat at his wife's bedside while she was dying. Their thirteen children fled in all directions in an effort to save themselves. While Hart lived in forests and caves for over a year, his home was burned and his business laid waste. He returned home to find his wife dead and his children and properties gone. He died shortly thereafter of grief and heartache.[109]

The fact of the matter is that these men pledged their lives, their fortunes, and their sacred honor. The price they paid for liberty and freedom is unsurpassable. They gladly gave up their well-established lives in exchange for a freedom they would never fully be able to experience. Is there anything you believe in enough that you would put your reputation and your life in jeopardy? At what point, as a Bible-believing Christian, will you object to the moral corruption being forced upon you, your children and future generations to come?

> *"If we abide by the principles taught in the*
> *Bible, our country will go on prospering and*
> *to prosper; but if we and our posterity neglect*
> *its instructions and authority, no man can tell*
> *how sudden a catastrophe may overwhelm us*
> *and bury all our glory in profound obscurity."*
> –DANIEL WEBSTER, 1821

Our Founding Fathers objected to a tea tax of one-half of one percent and gave their lives in return. Will we object if our children are routinely indoctrinated in a Marxist, America-hating, "gender fluid" ideology in our public schools? The Marxists have come out of the closet; why hasn't the church done the same?

Will we take a stand if imperfect babies are being killed in hospitals *after* they are born? Will we protest if the state tells our pastor what he can and cannot say from the pulpit? What if the state assumes "owner-ship" of children and tells parents how they must raise them—under penalty of losing custody? Will you take action then?

Will we argue if Christian businesses are required to satisfy a quota of gay, lesbian, and transgender employ-ees? Will the Church cry out if universities refuse to grant degrees to outspoken Christian students? Will we stand up and be heard when merely quoting Genesis 1:27—"male and female created He them"—is counted as a "hate crime"? Will we object when every tenet of our faith is legislated against in Congress? When will we begin to defend our rights and freedoms set forth in our Constitution?

All of the aforementioned are now in process in America. At what point will we have had enough? To make any compromise with the world is to be guilty of treason against God. James states that "friendship with the world is enmity with God" (James 4:4). When will we take action?

Listen to the echo coming from Valley Forge. Look at the American patriot—stained with blood, hungry, barefoot, standing in the snow with his musket firmly grasped. He fought in those conditions and now we are armed with the right to vote; yet, we sit at home on Election Day because the weather is bad.

That patriot left his family alone and destitute to allow us the freedom of speech; yet, we remain silent to avoid political incorrectness or repercussion. He orphaned his crying children in order for us to have a representative government, but through neglect we have allowed that government to become the master of our children and the murderer of the unborn.

> *"We have been assured, Sir, in the Sacred Writings, that 'except the Lord build, they labor in vain that build it.' I firmly believe this; and I also believe that without his concurring aid we shall succeed in this political building no better than the Builders of Babel."*
> —BENJAMIN FRANKLIN[110]

When the Continental Congress came to an impasse, Benjamin Franklin called upon the members of Congress to fall on their knees and ask God for guidance. He said, "We have been assured in the sacred writings (of the Bible) that except the Lord build, they labor in vain that built it." Do we labor in vain? Will America endure?

In *The Decline and Fall of the Roman Empire*, Edward Gibbon offers six reasons for Rome's collapse: rapid increase in divorce, belittling the sanctity of the home, higher taxes with public monies being wasted, mad craze for hedonistic pleasures, increased spending on armaments while the nation decayed internally, and the decline of faith in God that had become mere form.[111] Does any of this sound familiar? Do you see any reflection of these in our society today?

In the late eighteenth century Alexander Fraser Tytler, a Scottish history professor at the University of Edinburgh, had this to say about the fall of the Athenian republic some 2,000 years prior: "A democracy is always temporary in nature; it simply cannot exist as a permanent form of government. A democracy will continue to exist up until the time that voters discover they can vote themselves generous gifts from the public treasury." Tyler points out that from this moment on, the majority always votes for the candidates who promise the most benefits from the public treasury, the end result being collapse of the democracy with dictatorship soon to follow.[112]

*"Whereas it is fit and becoming in all people
at all times to acknowledge and revere the
supreme government of God; to bow in humble
submission to His chastisement to confess
and deplore their sins and transgressions in
the full conviction that the fear of the Lord is
the beginning of wisdom, and to pray, with
all fervency and contrition, for the pardon of
their past offenses and for a blessing upon
their present and prospective action . . ."*
–ABRAHAM LINCOLN[113]
PROCLAMATION 85, PROCLAIMING A DAY OF
NATIONAL HUMILIATION, PRAYER, AND FASTING
FOLLOWING THE BATTLE OF BULL RUN

Our nation celebrated its 244th birthday in 2020. From the beginning of history, the average age of the world's greatest civilizations has been about two hundred years. During those years, these great nations always progress through the following sequence: from bondage to spiritual faith; from spiritual faith to courage; from courage to liberty; from liberty to abundance; from abundance to complacency; from complacency to apathy; from apathy to dependence; from dependence back into bondage.[114]

As we look around, we can see that a significant percentage of the American populace has already entered the "dependence" phase of decline that immediately precedes bondage. But we can serve as a "saving remnant" for our nation. We can reverse that downward slide back into servitude.

So much is at stake in this election year. We must realize that our freedom is hanging in the balance and apathy threatens to wipe it out altogether. America's fate does not lie in the hands of politicians; it lies in the hands of God. The plain truth is that we, the people, have too-often put godless men and women in office. God will not cast our vote for us; we still have the free will to sit at home on Election Day.

As we cast our votes, we must vote for people with integrity, character, and a moral foundation. As believers, we may say "In God We Trust," but many times we walk into the voting booth and forget Biblical principles. Scripture states that " . . . when a wicked man rules, the people groan!" (Proverbs 29:2, NASB). It goes on to say, "Those who forsake the law praise the wicked, but those who keep the law strive with them" (Proverbs 28:4, NASB).

We can no longer sit idly by, convincing ourselves that our vote does not count. The one thing we have in common with the patriots who fought over two hundred years ago is the fact that we too are in a war in which the future of America hangs in the balance. That future is our cause, and time is up. God's people must stand up and speak up. The initiative lies solely with us. God responds to our choices. What we do here on earth with prayer and action determines what God can do for us in heaven.

God has given us the authority to make good choices for our land, and we have an obligation to make those choices. The Founding Fathers risked their lives and sacred honor in order for us to have a voice; we have a moral duty to cry out. Do not think that hope is lost; God will hear the cry of His children.

....

" . . . if my people who are called by My name shall humble themselves, and pray and seek My face, and turn from their wicked ways, then will I hear from heaven, and I will forgive their sin and heal their land."
–2 CHRONICLES 7:14

....

We must bear this responsibility and know that the future of America does not lie in the hands of the ungodly . . . it's in the hands of God's children. It is imperative that we always exercise our right to vote; we have everything to gain and so much to lose.

> *"Let each citizen remember at the moment*
> *he is offering his vote that he is not making*
> *a present or a compliment to please an*
> *individual—or at least that he ought not so*
> *to do; but that he is executing one of the most*
> *solemn trusts in human society for which*
> *he is accountable to God and his country."*
> —SAMUEL ADAMS[115]

The battle lines are now drawn. We must now prepare ourselves to make an impact on our society and be a good witness to those around us. Too many times in our society, Christians are being portrayed to be extremely judgmental, with nothing to offer society but criticism and negative attitudes. "Christianity is a great idea. Too bad no one has tried it." These words, spoken by a famous British playwright and cynic, Oscar Wilde, reflect an all too familiar stereotype regarding Christianity.

Bertrand Russell, the most famous atheist in the beginning of the twentieth century, said that, "The reason I am not a Christian is because I know too many Christians." Words like these are a tragic indictment of the followers of Jesus Christ; sadly enough in many cases they are true. Petty, judgmental, legalistic, and hypocritical people fill the pews of many of today's churches. It is those with scathing attitudes and actions that solicit such negative comments from people like Wilde, Russell and a large portion of society.

This cliché can no longer be perpetuated. We must accurately convey to society that, while we are a political force to be reckoned with, we are also a caring people that only want the best for our collective futures and the future of our children and grandchildren. A Christian's failure to "preach the gospel" with actions and deeds can cause people to repel from God and the gospel. If Christians are fueled by malice, greed, and judgment, the world will not receive what we have to say, rather they will be condemned for our hypocrisy.

Christians will not be able to change anything unless we change ourselves. We must demonstrate to society that we have something they want, something they are missing. We must convey to the world that Christianity is not something to be endured, but something to be treasured. Instead of legalism, we must offer them life; instead of liturgy, we must offer them liberty; and instead of loathing, we must offer them love.

With the current moral climate in the world today, people should be standing in line to get into church. We need to give them a reason to do so. We must change our lives to reflect Christ in us, let our light shine, and change the world.

This is our challenge, a challenge for which we will be accountable to the Lord Jesus Christ, whom we serve. Will we have brought improvement to the world, healing to mankind, or will we allow the darkness to envelop us and create more darkness in the process? Our Creator gives us a choice. If not now, when? If not us, then who?

Political Involvement

"Nothing is so fatal to religion as indifference
which is, at least, half infidelity"
–EDMUND BURKE[116]

Burke claims that "indifference" is fatal to religion; the same can be said of the political process. To be apathetic toward the laws that control your life and the lives of your children is to be an unfaithful American. We need to do more than cast our vote. We need to set the terms of debate and let our voices be heard. We must start in our own communities and let our influence at home be heard all the way to the White House.

Usually when you ask most people to name an elective office, virtually everyone will say president, vice-president, senator, governor, or other high-profile offices. People forget that there are precinct elections after every primary election, and that the results of these precinct caucuses shape the agenda of the state party conventions later in that year. At the precinct meeting, which is held after the polls close at the same location where you voted, your neighbors will elect delegates to the county or district convention and will vote on resolutions to be proposed for the party platform.

This process is repeated at the county or district level, where delegates to the state convention are elected and recommendations for the party platform are debated and voted upon. At the state convention, delegates to the national convention are elected, and at the national convention the final version of the party platform is adopted. It's possible for a resolution started by average citizens at a precinct meeting to travel all the way to the national party convention where the party's presidential nominee is selected.

Political parties are like any other organization. Organizational loyalty, frequency of participation in party events, and longevity of association all count for influence in a political party. One of the unique aspects of our American political structure—which for all its weakness is hailed as the best in the world—is that plain, average persons are not only allowed to vote, but also to have a larger impact in the political process.

Political involvement goes further than casting a vote. Edmund Burke, political philosopher and states-man, once said, "It is a general popular error to suppose the loudest complainers for the public to be the most anxious for its welfare."[117] We must do more than stand on our soapbox and complain. We will not be acknowl-edged for the problems we recognize, but for the problems we help solve.

We can all get involved in the political process by volunteering in local campaigns, making financial contributions to a worthy candidate, fundraising, or supporting voter registration drives. Involvement can be taken even further by trying to influence opin-ion in public forums by writing letters to the editor of newspapers and calling into radio talk shows to voice our informed opinion, bringing to the surface issues that are important to sustain traditional values in America. We can even run for precinct or county offices. Somebody has to fill the lower offices in our system, so why not us?

Elective offices in our nation periodically open up for the general population to once again vote for candidates they believe will best represent their value systems as they fulfill the governmental powers accorded the office. Someone has to run—someone will—and someone will be elected. Why can't that someone be a person who loves Jesus Christ and who considers their governmental position to be a sacred trust? Our nation is a sum of its parts; it can only be as good as the individuals who live in it and lead it. We are those individuals. What are we doing to make our nation be the best it can be? If not us ... then who? If not now ... when?

> *"The only thing necessary for the triumph*
> *of evil is for good men to do nothing."*
> —EDMUND BURKE[118]

Casting Your Vote

In the Sermon on the Mount, Jesus not only told His followers that they were the light of the world, He also said they were the salt of the earth (see Matthew 5:13). Salt is meant to season and to preserve. It is important for us to be the "salt" that seasons our communities with moral virtue as prescribed in the Word of God. It is equally important to take seriously the preservation function of "salt" by translating the truth into votes.

First, we must understand that, as Bible-believing Christians, our views and our political priorities will always be unpopular. Most people are not going to agree with us on everything. The Lord reminds us that the way to heaven is through a "narrow gate" and "there are few who find it" (Matthew 7:13–14). Believers are often going to be outnumbered; and if we are to prevail, we must stick together, and each do our part to stand for righteousness. That makes it doubly important that each Christian register and get involved in the political process. Above all, it is critical that we not just register but that we go to the polls and cast our vote. The only tangible way Jesus Christ is going to have a "voice" in each election is for each follower to express that voice by means of prayerfully casting a ballot on the issues.

While the decision to change can be made in the space of a moment of prayer, changing governmental structures and the way people vote can take years. Here at the cusp of change in an election year, we have two major political parties in America. One is the home where most advocate homosexuality, abortion, maximum taxation, unlimited handouts, and little freedom from government control. The other major party is the home of social conservatives who for the most part believe in the sanctity of life, hard work, clean moral living, limited government interference, minimum taxation, and a return to Bible-based societal values. We as Christians must choose our party and our candidates based on our convictions dictated in the Word of God.

The way to keep a political party accountable to their constituents is to go to the ballot box. Because so many do not cast their vote on Election Day, in many cases Americans end up being governed by a relatively small percentage of the population. For example, during the 2020 primary campaign in Texas it was estimated that a mere three percent of registered voters would determine the result for the other 97 percent of the people that didn't bother to vote in the primary. If people of righteousness would see to it that there was a candidate running in each election who shared our godly values, and if all Christians voted for that person, then America would have an opportunity to climb out of the moral decline we have experienced in the last several decades.

God's Candidate for America

With liberty, morality, decency, and religious freedom under assault on every side, it is our responsibility to stand up and speak out for the traditional values that made America the greatest nation in the world. Qualified Christians should: stand for elective office; seek out and serve as appointed officials whenever possible; and see to it that our children receive a higher education so that they will be qualified to lead the next generation.

In a nation of 330 million people, there is no reason to tolerate unrighteousness in our governmental offices. With only 535 seats in Congress, one president, one vice-president, and 50 governors, why should we ever settle for less than what is required by God Himself. "Righteousness exalts a nation, but sin is a reproach to any people" (Proverbs 14:34). The apostle Paul wrote to the Corinthian believers that all Christians are "ambassadors for Christ" (2 Corinthians 5:20). An ambassador is an official representative of a specific government. We must be Christ's ambassadors in the voting booth, and there is no time like the present to start. If we want to be the salt of the earth, if we want to let our light shine, if we want to make a difference in this nation, we must not be afraid to take a stand and legislate morality that will help shape society for the better. If we do not, someone else will, and they will control your fate. We must choose God's candidate for America.

In 1832, Noah Webster spoke on the importance of voting. Almost prophetically he has painted the face of American voters and what their apathy has meant to our political system. He states:

> "When you become entitled to exercise the right of voting for public officers, let it be impressed upon your mind that God commands you to choose for rulers, 'just men who will rule in the fear of God.' The preservation of government depends on the faithful discharge of this duty; if the citizens neglect their duty and place unprincipled men in office, the government will soon be corrupted; laws will be made, not for the public good so much as for selfish or local purposes; corrupt or incompetent men will be appointed to execute the laws; and the rights of the citizens will be violated or disregarded. If a republican government fails to secure public prosperity and happiness, it must be because the citizens neglect the divine commands, and elect bad men to administer the laws."[119]

We must unite to preserve our form of government and our way of life. We must understand exactly what is at stake when we step into a voting booth. We will only have as much freedom as we are willing to fight for. We must unite and we must fight, because our future depends on it. The Lord says in the book of Jeremiah 9:23–24:

> ... *"Let not the wise man glory in his wisdom, let not the mighty man glory in his might, nor let the rich man glory in his riches; but let him who glories glory in this, that he understands and knows Me, that I am the Lord, exercising lovingkindness, judgment, and righteousness in the earth. For in these I delight," says the Lord.*

The Lord delights in justice and righteousness. Through the miracle of America's founding, He has given us the ability to choose righteousness in the voting booth. Too many have sacrificed too much blood, sweat, and treasure for us to see it all swept away in a godless tide humanistic deception.

We must wake up and take action! Our future is at stake. Our posterity must not be sacrificed on the altar of political corruption and socialism. We must stand up, speak up, and vote the values of the Bible.

APPENDIX A

Guidelines for Church and Clergy

There has been much confusion as to what a church and Pastor can and can't do. The following are guidelines intended to direct civic leaders to do what is legal under the law. These guidelines were taken and influenced by materials distributed through Concerned Women for America.

1. **A church can educate its members on issues that affect the moral condition of the country, the education of our children, and the involvement of its members in the political process.**

A church can educate the congregation by preaching from the pulpit, teaching in Sunday school classes, sponsoring seminars on topics such as Bible positions on political issues, and providing literature for distribution of educational materials.

Another way to educate its members is by hosting or conducting a nonpartisan candidate forum in which candidates debate or discuss their views on relevant issues of interest to the general public. All candidates for a particular office in question should be invited to participate to avoid bias for or against any particular candidate or party.

2. **A church can participate in "legislative activity" as long as it does not exceed 5% of the overall**

activity of the church's programs. Anything over 5% has either been questioned or held unacceptable under section 501(c)3 of the Internal Revenue Code.

"Legislative activity" is defined as any conduct intended to influence legislation—-bills before the U.S. Congress and state legislatures, measures before city councils, initiatives and referendums. These cover actions such as contacting legislators about legislation, urging church members and others to communicate with legislators about legislation, and circulating petitions related to specific legislation.

3. A church can engage in voter registration and voter education projects such as "get-out-the-vote" drives. The church may spend money to pay registration organizers or to mail out registration forms. You may contact your local voter registration office for forms and procedures.

The voter registration drive must be nonpartisan, not showing any bias for or against a candidate or political party. No display of campaign materials on specific issues that will create a bias for or against a certain candidate, or urge voters to register for a particular party, should be present.

4. A church may not endorse or oppose a candidate for public office. Additionally, when a Pastor is speaking on behalf of his church, he cannot endorse or oppose a candidate for public office.

5. A pastor of a church may, as an individual, personally endorse or oppose a candidate. This endorsement should occur on personal time and not from his pulpit to prevent the endorsement from being attributed to the church.

Additionally, if a pastor lends his name to a candidate for political advertisements or devotes personal time to a candidate's campaign, his title may be listed with his name for the purpose of identification. The fact that a church employs the pastor does not negate his constitutional rights of free speech and political expression.

6. Candidates may be introduced to a congregation in the course of a service. In addition, candidates may be allowed to preach, teach, and read scriptures on the same basis as other church members or participants. However, a candidate should not be allowed to deliver political speeches to gain support or raise funds for his campaign.

7. A church may not contribute money or raise funds for a political party or a candidate for public office. If the church is incorporated, the Federal Election Campaign Act prohibits any corporation from making contributions or expenditures in connection with a federal campaign.

8. Candidates should not be allowed to use church facilities or property for political purposes because it may be viewed equivalent to a contribution.

9. A church may not loan its membership or mailing list to a candidate or political committee for use in an election campaign.

10. A church may distribute voter guides educating their members on the voting records of all candidates running for office. A voter guide should report the views of all candidates by publishing their public records or publishing their responses to unbiased, nonpartisan questionnaires.

Our nation and our government are in desperate need of the "salt and light" that only the Church, her pastors, and her people can provide. By understanding and creatively using the lawful means at our disposal, we can make a difference!

(This information is intended to initiate a general discussion and should not be interpreted as a legal devise. Churches or pastors needing advice on a particular circumstance should ask the counsel of their own legal or tax advisors.)

APPENDIX B

Other Informational Resources

Federal Election Commission
Register to vote online at:
www.fec.gov

Family Research Council (FRC)
www.frc.org
This is an invaluable source of statistics and
information on family policy issues.

Contact Your Senator
https://www.senate.gov/general/contact_information/
senators_cfm.cfm
Starting petitions on issues in your church and
neighborhoods makes a huge impact.

Contact Your Congressman
www.house.gov

Tools for Letter Writing and Voting Records
How to write a letter to your Congressman:
https://www.wikihow.com/Address-a-Letter-to-
a-Government-Official

Recorded Votes on the House and Senate Floor:
https://www.govtrack.us/congress/votes

Good Sources for Information, Polls, Studies, and Tools for Conservative Voters

The Heritage Foundation:
https://www.heritage.org/

The Washington Free Beacon:
https://freebeacon.com/

The American Thinker:
https://www.americanthinker.com/

National Review:
https://www.nationalreview.com/

TheBlaze:
https://www.theblaze.com/

PJ Media:
https://pjmedia.com/

Twitchy:
https://twitchy.com/

RedState:
https://www.redstate.com/

LifeSiteNews.com:
https://www.lifesitenews.com/

The Federalist:
https://thefederalist.com/

The Daily Wire:
https://www.dailywire.com/

RealClearPolitics:
https://www.realclearpolitics.com/ (Not a "conservative" website, but a good source of current political information.)

WORKS CITED

1   Gottschalk, Jonah, "List Of 183 Monuments Ruined Since Protests Began, And Counting." *The Federalist*, July 22, 2020. (https://thefederalist.com/2020/07/22/list-of-183-monuments-ruined-since-protests-began-and-counting/)

2   Holland, Tom, *Dominion: How the Christian Revolution Remade the World*, Hachette: New York, 2019. p. 13

3   Cantor, Eric. "What the Obama Presidency Looked Like to the Opposition". *New York Times* (January 14, 2017) (https://www.nytimes.com/2017/01/14/opinion/sunday/eric-cantor-what-the-obama-presidency-looked-like-to-the-opposition.html)

4   Genesis 1:28

5   Hill, Napoleon. *Think and Grow Rich*. London, England: Penguin Group, 2005, p. 103

6   Ecclesiastes 4:8-7

7   Psalm 127:3

8   https://en.wikipedia.org/wiki/2008_California_Proposition_8

9   *Roe v. Wade*, 410 U.S. 113 (1973)

10   *Obergefell v. Hodges*, 576 U.S. (2015)

11   Ibid.

12   Ibid.

13   http://srdiocese.org/content/justice-samuel-alito%E2%80%99s-dissent-obergefell-v-hodges-decision

14   Hasson, Peter. "Facebook, Amazon, Google And Twitter All Work With Left-Wing SPLC." Daily Caller News Foundation, June 6, 2018. (https://dailycaller.com/2018/06/06/splc-partner-google-facebook-amazon/)

15   Kabbany, Jennifer. "Move over LGBTQ, the new acronym is LGBTTQQFAGPBDSM (No, this is not a joke)." The College Fix. (http://www.thecollegefix.com/post/21404/?utm_source=feedburner&utm_medium=feed&utm_campaign=Feed%3A+

thecollegefixfeed+%28The+College+Fix%29)

16 Killermann, Sam. "Breaking through the Binary: Gender As a
    Continuum." Issues Magazine, June 2014.

17 Sorto, Gabrielle. "A teacher says he was fired for refusing to use
    male pronouns for a transgender student." CNN.com, October 2,
    2019. (https://www.cnn.com/2019/10/02/us/virginia-teacher-says-
    wrongfully-fired-student-wrong-pronouns-trnd/index.html)

18 Mandel, Bethany. "Sorry, but men cannot have periods." The
    Washington Examiner, November 7, 2019. (https://www.washington
    examiner.com/opinion/sorry-but-men-cannot-have-periods)

19 https://twitter.com/CNN/status/1288948978088804355?s=20

20 McLanahan, Sara and Harper, Cynthia. "Father Absence and
    Youth Incarceration." Journal of Research on Adolescence,
    August 16, 2004. (https://onlinelibrary.wiley.com/doi/
    abs/10.1111/j.1532 7795.2004.00079.x)

21 "One-Parent Families and Their Children." Charles F.
    Kettering Foundation, 1990. (https://www.liveabout.com/
    fatherless-children-in-america-statistics-1270392)

22 Parker, Wayne. "Statistics on Fatherless Children in
    America." May 24, 2019. (https://www.liveabout.com/
    fatherless-children-in-america statistics-1270392)

23 Whitehead, Barbara Dafoe. Before the Senate Subcommittee on
    Children and Families. U.S. Senate, April 28, 2004.

24 Transcript of Gretchen Ritter posted on The Colson Center website,
    BreakPoint. "A Strange Take on Stay-at-Home Moms." Commentary
    #040727, July 27, 2004.

25 Ibid.

26 Alcorn, Randy. ProLife Answers to ProChoice Arguments. Multnomah
    Books: Colorado Springs, CO, 2000. p. 57

27 Epstein, Lee and Thomas G. Walker. Constitutional Law for a
    Changing America: A Short Course. p.432

28 Ibid. p. 57

29 Scott v. Sanford 19 How (60. U.S.) 393 (1857)

30 Ed., "Unborn Children as Constitutional Persons", National Library of Medicine, https://pubmed.ncbi.nlm.nih.gov/20443281/

31 https://www.landmarkcases.org/roe-v-wade/roe-v-wade-summary-of-the-decision#:~:text=Roe%20v.-,Wade%3A%20Summary%20of%20the%20Decision,and%20Douglas%20wrote%20concurring%20opinions.

32 Alcorn, Randy. *ProLife Answers to ProChoice Arguments*. Multnomah Books: Colorado Springs, CO, 2000. p.46

33 https://www.landmarkcases.org/roe-v-wade/roe-v-wade-summary-of-the-decision#:~:text=Roe%20v.-,Wade%3A%20Summary%20of%20the%20Decision,and%20Douglas%20wrote%20concurring%20opinions.

34 Butler, Stuart M. and Kim R. Holmes. *Issues 2000: The Candidates Briefing Book*. The Heritage Foundation. February 15, 2000. p. 212.

35 Budziszewski, J. *The Revenge of Conscience: Politics and the Fall of Man*. WIPF and STOCK Publishers: Eugene, Ohio, 2010.

36 Ibid p. 21

37 Ibid p. 21

38 Stubblefield, Phillip G. "First and Second Trimester Abortion." Gynecologic and Obstetric Surgery, ed. David H. Nichols. Baltimore: Mosby, 1993. p. 1016

39 U.S. Center for Disease Control (CDC), "Abortion Surveillance: Preliminary Data-United States, 1991" Morbidity and Mortality Report, Vol. 43, No, 1994. p. 43

40 Hern, M.D., Warren M. *Abortion Practice*. Philadelphia: J.B. Lippincott & Company, 1984. pp.153-154

41 Haskell. Dr. Martin. "Second Trimester D&X, 20 Weeks and Beyond." National Abortion Federation, *Second Trimester Abortion: From Every Angle*, 1992. pp. 29-31

42 Ibid pp. 15-16

43 Stout, David. *"An Abortion Rights Advocate Says He Lied About Procedure."* New York Times, Feb. 26, 1997.

44 Ibid.

45 Anad, Dr. Kanawaljeet S. (fetal pain expert) *Excerpt from report to U.S. Federal Court regarding Partial Birth Act.* January 15, 2004. pp. 5-6

46 Ibid.

47 Johnson, Douglas. "The Partial-Birth Abortion Ban Act- Misconceptions and Realities." November 5, 2003. p.3 (http://www. nrlc.org/archive/abortion/pba/PBAall110403.html)

48 Schindehette, Susan. "Against All Odds." *People Magazine*, July 19, 2004. (https://people.com/archive/against-all-odds-vol-62-no-3/)

49 Budziszewski, J. *The Revenge of Conscience: Politics and the Fall of Man.* WIPF and STOCK Publishers: Eugene, Ohio, 2010.

50 Kirsanow, Peter. "Clarifying Obama's Vote on Born-Alive." *National Review*, February 10, 2012 (https://www.nationalreview.com/corner/ clarifying-obamas-vote-born-alive-peter-kirsanow/)

51 Sowell, Thomas. "Is Reality Optional?: And Other Essays." Hoover Institution Press, 1993.

52 https://burningdesireforfire.com/ lessons-from-literature-7-one-day-in-the-life-of-ivan-denisovich/

53 http://www.let.rug.nl/usa/documents/1776-1785/the-final-text-of- the-declaration-of-independence-july-4-1776.php

54 Sowell, Thomas. "The 'Equality' Racket." Jewish World Review, January 6, 2015 (http://jewishworldreview.com/cols/sowell010615. php3)

55 Sowell, Thomas. *Wealth, Poverty and Politics: An International Perspective*, Hachette Publishing, 2016

56 http://www.wilberforceacademy.org/blog/2019/2/27/ why-the-social-justice-tidal-wave-in-evangelical-churches

57 Statement made by Margaret Thatcher during an interview with journalist Llew Gardner for Thames Television's *This Week* program on 5 February 1976.

58 The Constitution of the United States of America. *(Establishment Clause and Free Exercise Clause of the 1st Amendment, ratified December 15, 1791.)*

59 Geisler, Dr. Norman & Frank Turek. *Legislating Morality*, 1998 p.18

60 James Madison, Alexander Hamilton, and John Jay, *The Federalist Papers*, Number 39 and 51: First published in 1788.

61 http://www.let.rug.nl/usa/documents/1776-1785/the-final-text-of-the-declaration-of-independence-july-4-1776.php

62 Ibid. p.58

63 *The Oxford Desk Dictionary*, 1995: p. 273

64 Psalm 2:1–3 (NIV)

65 "Judicial Jihad," World Net Daily, posted December 13, 2003. www.world-netdaily.com

66 *Thomas More Law Center v. Byron Union School District* (2003)

67 Limbaugh, David. Persecution: *How Liberals Are Waging War Against Christians*. Regnery: Washington, DC, 2003. Chapter 1

68 Rice, Harvey. "Lawsuit Claims Students Not Allowed to Carry Bibles" *Houston Chronicle*, May 23, 2000

69 "School Assignment: Open Discussion of Christmas But Not Allowed to Mention Christ." Boston Globe, July 30, 2002. (Posted on www.underreported.com, August 2,2002.)

70 Ibid.

71 Larry Mundinger et al. "Judge Ira Dement Issues New Warning in Alabama Prayer Case," November 17, 1997 www.positiveatheism.com

72 Ibid.

73 Castellon, Michael. "Controversy Arises from Professors Policy" *The University Daily*, October 24, 2002 (For more information, go to: http://www.dailytoreador.com/archives/controversy-arises-from-professors-policy/article_b02c05f8-6090-5bb7-bf2a-b0dae29a951e.html)

74 "A Truly Multicultural Society," October 2000 (An email exchange between George Marsden and *The Atlantic's* Wen Stephenson; www.theatlantic.com.)

75 Colson, Charles. *Against the Night: Living in the New Dark Ages*. 1989, p.85

76 *Halley's Bible Handbook*. Zondervan, 1965. pp18–19

77 Abraham Lincoln Quotes. BrainyQuote.com, BrainyMedia Inc, 2020. https://www.brainyquote.com/quotes/abraham_lincoln_133687, accessed August 11, 2020.

78 Proverbs 22:6

79 Potter, Charles Francis. *Humanism: A New Religion*, 1930. p. 128

80 Kurtz, Paul & Edwin H. Wilson. *"Humanist Manifesto II."* The Humanist, September/October 1973 (Vol. XXXIII, No. 5)

81 McDonough, Siobhan. "Religion embedded in U.S. society, government, courts" *The Washington Times*, August 24, 2003 (https://www.washingtontimes.com/news/2003/aug/23/20030823-112754-1898r/)

82 "Moses Image (With 10 Commandments) Adorns U.S. Supreme Court Building."August 20, 2003 (http://www.freerepublic.com/focus/news/967509/posts?page=139)

83 Ibid.

84 https://www.facebook.com/OKFaithLeaders/ posts/1176904585990519

85 https://constitution.congress.gov/constitution/ amendment-1/#:~:text=Constitution%20of%20the%20United%20 States&text=Congress%20shall%20make%20no%20law,for%20 a%20redress%20of%20grievances.

86 Ibid. Epstein and Walker, p. 427

87 Ibid.

88 Thomas Jefferson, Thomas. Letter to William Johnson, June 12, 1823. *The Complete Jefferson*, p. 322 (Madison & Adams Press, 2018. info@madisonadamspress.com)

89 Ibid. Geisler & Turek p. 16

90 Ibid. p. 24

91 Psalm 2:2, 4 (NASB)

92 Adapted from the CUFI eBook "Why Christians Should Support Israel"

93 Larkin, Rev. Clarence. Charts from the book of Dispensational Truth. January 18, 1919, Glenside, PA, Larkin Estate

94 https://www.israelhayom.com/2020/06/02/

bds-co-founder-says-goal-of-movement-is-end-of-israel/

95 https://www.huffpost.com/entry/
hm-offensive-shirt-star-of-david_n_5034603

96 https://www.cnn.com/2019/12/04/europe/france-jewish-
cemetery-swastikas-intl/index.html

97 https://www.timesofisrael.com/french-soccer-player-uses-
nazi-like-quenelle-salute-to-celebrate-goal/

98 Hagee, John. *In Defense of Israel*. Charisma Media: Lake Mary,
Florida, 2007

99 Diary of John Adams, February 22, 1756.
(http://www.foundingfatherquotes.com/quote/1282)

100 Staff, "In U.S., Decline of Christianity Continues at Rapid
Pace", Pew Research Center: Religion and Public Life,
October 17, 2019 (https://www.pewforum.org/2019/10/17/
in-u-s-decline-of-christianity-continues-at-rapid-pace/)

101 https://www.heritage.org/poverty-and-inequality/report/
the-war-poverty-after-50-years

102 Tyrell, Patrick. Heritage Foundation, (2015),
https://www.heritage.org/welfare/commentary/
one-measure-955-million-are-dependent-the-federal-government

103 President George Washington's THANKSGIVING PROCLAMATION,
City of New York, October 3, 1789.

104 https://www.life.church/media/problem-or-a-miracle/
problem-or-a-miracle/

105 Belmonte, Kevin. "Steadfast Companions: The Story of Clapham
Circle." December 2003

106 *Church of the Holy Trinity v. United States*, U.S. Supreme Court, 1892.

107 Paul Harvey, "The Rest of the Story: Our Lives, Our Fortunes, and
Our Sacred Honor." 1956

108 Ibid.

109 Ibid.

110 Statement made at the Constitutional Convention, June 28, 1787.
Also, introduced in the Senate on May 23, 2006 to commemorate

the 50th anniversary of its formal adoption. (Congressional Bills 109th Congress, from the U.S. Government Publishing Office, S. Con. Res. 96, May 23, 2006. https://www.govinfo.gov/content/pkg/BILLS-109sconres96is/html/BILLS-109sconres96is.htm)

111 Gibbon, Edward. "General Observations on the Fall of the Roman Empire in the West." *(Posted on June 15, 1999 http://ancienthistory.about.com)*

112 Tytler, Alexander Fraser, Lord Woodhouselee. *The Fall of the Athenian Republic*, 1787

113 https://www.presidency.ucsb.edu/documents/proclamation-85-proclaiming-day-national-humiliation-prayer-and-fasting

114 Ibid.

115 Adams, Samuel. *The Writings of Samuel Adams*, Harry Alonzo Cushing, editor (New York: G.P. Putnam's Sons, 1907), Vol. IV, p. 256, in the *Boston Gazette* on April 16, 1781.

116 Burke, Peter. *The Wisdom and Genius of the Right Hon. Edmund Burke: Illustrated in a Series of Extracts from His Writings and Speeches; with a Summary of His Life*, January 8, 2010. pp. 218–219

117 Ibid.

118 Ibid.

119 Posted on Chuck Colson's commentary, "A Sacred Duty: Why Christians Must Vote" May 14, 2004 (www.townhall.com)

ABOUT THE AUTHOR

PASTOR JOHN C. HAGEE is the founder and Senior Pastor of Cornerstone Church in San Antonio, Texas, a non-denominational evangelical church with more than 22,000 active members. Pastor Hagee has served the Lord in the gospel ministry for over 60 years.

Pastor Hagee received a Bachelor of Science degree from Southwestern Assemblies of God University in Waxahachie, Texas and a second Bachelor of Science degree from Trinity University in San Antonio, Texas. He earned his Master's Degree in Educational Administration from the University of North Texas in Denton, Texas.

He has received Honorary Doctorates from Oral Roberts University, Canada Christian College, and Netanya Academic College of Israel.

Pastor Hagee is the author of 40 major books, seven of which were on *The New York Times* Bestseller's List.

He is the founder of *Hagee Ministries*, which telecasts his teachings throughout America and the nations of the world. Over the years, *Hagee Ministries* has given more than $100 million toward humanitarian causes in Israel.

Pastor Hagee is the founder of Cornerstone Christian Schools that just completed a $100 million dollar campus which holds 2,400 students and is committed to providing a Bible-based education to future generations.

He is the founder of the Sanctuary of Hope, a multi-million dollar facility that gives young, pregnant mothers a home to raise their children rather than aborting them. This home gives the opportunity of life to children that would have otherwise been killed in abortion clinics.

Pastor Hagee is the founder and National Chairman of *Christians United For Israel* (CUFI), a grass-roots organization which has grown to become the largest Christian pro-Israel group in the United States with over 7 million members that speak as one voice on behalf of Israel.

John Hagee was recognized by the state of Israel on its 70th Anniversary as one of the 70 greatest contributors to Israel since statehood. He was also invited by U.S. Ambassador David Friedman to give the benediction at the opening of the U.S. Embassy in Jerusalem.

Pastor Hagee and his wife Diana are blessed with five children and thirteen grandchildren.